The Other Side of Me

Keith Hughes

THE OTHER SIDE OF ME

Keith Hughes

Pearly Gates Publishing LLC
INSPIRING CHRISTIAN AUTHORS TO BE AUTHORS
Pearly Gates Publishing, LLC, Houston, Texas

The Other Side of Me

The Other Side of Me

Copyright © 2019
Keith Hughes

All Rights Reserved.
No portion of this publication may be reproduced, stored in any electronic system, or transmitted in any form or by any means (electronic, mechanical, photocopy, recording, or otherwise) without written permission from the author or publisher. Brief quotations may be used in literary reviews.

ISBN 13: 978-1-947445-52-9
Library of Congress Control Number: 2019935869

Scripture references are taken from the King James Version (KJV), New American Standard Bible (NASB), New Century Version (NCV), New International Version (NIV), and The Living Bible (TLB) versions of the Holy Bible and are used with permission by Zondervan via Biblegateway.com Public Domain.

For information and bulk ordering, contact:
Pearly Gates Publishing, LLC
Angela R. Edwards, CEO
P.O. Box 62287
Houston, TX 77205
BestSeller@PearlyGatesPublishing.com

Keith Hughes

Dedication

In loving memory of my Dad,

Sylvester Hughes,

Shelley Renee Cotton,

and my good friend, *Chris Pavey.*

You are all loved and missed.

The Other Side of Me

Special Thanks To:

The Matriarch of our family, my mom, **Eirgie Lee Hughes**: Thank you for your love and for introducing us to Jesus Christ at an early age.

My wife, **Joann**: I love you more than words can say. I thank God for your support and patience in allowing me to pursue this project. As I've said before, I am so blessed to have you by my side.

My sons, **Adrian and Michael**: I am so blessed to have you guys in my life. It's an honor to be your dad. I can't wait to see what God has in store for you. Stay focused and positive.

My **siblings, nieces, nephews, and extended family**: I love you for always encouraging me to be the best that I can be. I have the best family in the world!

Pastor Phillip L. McPheeters & Life Changers Church, Evangelist Joyce Bryant, and Mother Emma Zelle Moody: Thank you for your endless love and wisdom. I am grateful for your teachings and, most of all, your friendship. I love you all. Be blessed!

The **River of Life Church family and Bishop John C. Williams**: I love you dearly. Thank you for your love and for welcoming me home.

A special acknowledgement to the **Rose of Sharon Church of God**: Thank you for your love and guidance. This is where it all started for me.

Prologue

While writing this book, I battled with sharing a lot of information for fear it would ruffle some feathers. I became more interested in protecting the interests of others rather than liberating myself from the issues that have plagued me since childhood. I thought about the impact it might bring, but quickly realized this book is about **MY** life; not anyone else's.

As I began my research of events, I realized early on that I was becoming a "discreet writer"—one who writes an intriguing, juicy story, only to leave out the most integral parts that make up a great storyline and leaves the reader guessing about what's to come. In essence, I was giving half-truths.

The Other Side of Me is a story of self-discovery, self-liberation, the breaking of generational curses, and facing fears that have left me asking, **"Why, God? Why ME?"**

This book was also designed to serve as an antidote for healing and deliverance and to give the reader a blueprint on how to forgive oneself and others who have caused hurt and pain. As well, it is intended to destroy generational curses with God's help, all while building a better future for the reader.

I refuse to go to my grave without having dealt with these issues. I don't think I would've ever been able to forgive myself had I not written this book. This was my way of healing mentally and spiritually—and then moving onto greater things in life. It is my prayer that whoever reads this book would be able to approach their fears head-on and find an encouraging resolution and spiritual uplifting that speaks volumes to their life.

This book is not designed to point fingers at anyone. I do not play the "Blame Game" here. Neither do I profess to be a victim. Rather, this writing is to serve as an avenue to show you how to take ownership of your life—whether you were dealt a bad hand or not—and ultimately see that in the end, you didn't lose. You will be able to say that you came out of the storm **VICTORIOUS!**

I need to free myself from this "cage of fear." My strongholds became my "Mask of Deception." This is my moment of truth! *The Other Side of Me* is not a figment of my imagination. It is real!

"I had become afraid of what I didn't understand…life and fear."

~ Author Keith Hughes ~

Introduction

Spiritual Strongholds:

"For the weapons of our warfare are not carnal, but mighty through God to the pulling down of strongholds; casting down imaginations, and every high thing that exalteth itself against the knowledge of God, and bringing into captivity every thought to the obedience of Christ."
(2 Corinthians 10:4-5)

A "stronghold" is an area of darkness within our mind or personality that causes ongoing spiritual, emotional, and behavioral problems. We can be genuinely born-again and sincere in our faith but have an ongoing struggle with thoughts, emotions, and habits that wage war against our relationship with Christ. We pray. We study. And we attempt to discipline ourselves, but often find our "problem" is our resistance to real change.

Memories:

People who suffer emotional trauma are prime candidates for spiritual strongholds. Ongoing memories of painful events prepare the heart to accept the suggestions of the 'Darkness.' If we're preoccupied with our painful past, then we will not be able to grow in faith or possess and walk out of new identity in Christ.

The Other Side of Me

Painful memories can and will drive us to bitterness, hatred, anxiety, or depression, but the Word of God will bring us healing. Even when we forgive the person or people who have hurt us, if the painful memories continue to recycle, then we can remain under the influence of those memories.

Jesus Gives a Sound Mind:

Christ gives us a sound mind, which means we are given the ability to see life with a healthy self-image. We have memories and do not forget the past; however, in Christ, we do not allow the past to control our new life. We put on the 'New Man' who is not controlled by the pains of the past.

Keep your faith. Lay hold on eternal life. Put to death fleshly lusts that wage war against the soul. The Lord is at hand, and everything that can be shaken will be shaken. Judgment must be given at the House of God. Keep yourself spotless before the world so that at His coming, you may be found in peace — blameless and without a spot or wrinkle. The wages of sin is death, but the gift of God is eternal life through Jesus Christ our Lord!

Table of Contents

DEDICATION	VI
SPECIAL THANKS TO:	VII
PROLOGUE	VIII
INTRODUCTION	X
CHAPTER ONE: GROWING UP IN TOLEDO, OHIO	1
CHAPTER TWO: LIFE LESSONS TO LIVE BY	6
CHAPTER THREE: GETTING THROUGH SCHOOL	14
CHAPTER FOUR: MY FIRST EXPOSURE TO PORNOGRAPHY	17
CHAPTER FIVE: THE MOVE TO CINCINNATI	26
CHAPTER SIX: THE BIRTH OF MY SON AND THE MUSIC BUSINESS	30
CHAPTER SEVEN: REASONS GOD REMOVES PEOPLE FROM YOUR LIFE	57
CHAPTER EIGHT: TUGGING AT THE SKIRT TAIL OF MY SISTER	78
CHAPTER NINE: DEALING WITH FEAR AND REJECTION	81
CHAPTER TEN: INTRODUCING MY SECRET TO MY PARENTS	99
CHAPTER ELEVEN: FIGHTING FEAR	106
CHAPTER TWELVE: WALKING AWAY FROM MY SPIRITUAL COVERING	117
CHAPTER THIRTEEN: THE ABUSIVE RELATIONSHIP	122
CHAPTER FOURTEEN: THE DAY I SERVED THE DEVIL HIS WALKING PAPERS	137
CHAPTER FIFTEEN: THE DEMONIC SUICIDE ATTACK	150
CHAPTER SIXTEEN: DISTRACTIONS	162
THERE IS LIFE AFTER THIS	183
ABOUT THE AUTHOR	186
APPENDIX	188

Chapter One

Growing Up in Toledo, Ohio

I grew up in Toledo, Ohio during the 1970s and 80s when children spent very little time inside the house. There was always something to do, no matter what the climate was. My siblings and I spent a considerable amount of time repairing old bikes, building wooden go-carts, picking green apples, cherries, and apricots out of the neighbor's trees, and standing in the alley throwing rocks at other kids.

The funny thing that I remember about growing up is that in the summertime, I would wear a red winter coat to play in. That's right; I wore a winter coat in the scorching, hot sun. Although it was hotter than Jerusalem in that coat, it was most comforting to me. I was fascinated with the comic book superheroes Batman & Robin, Superman, and the Incredible Hulk—and with saving the world. As wild as that may sound, that was, indeed, my reality.

My brothers and sisters thought I was weird and tried talking me out of wearing my red coat in the heat. It didn't work! It never failed that once our summer breaks were over and it was time for us to return to school, I could never find my coat during the winter months.

Keith Hughes

So, one day, while playing outside, my dad was working on one of his old trucks in the backyard, and he called me over. In a very calm voice, he asked, *"Son, why the heck is your wearing that coat – as hot as it is out here? Go in the house and take it off!"* As I turned to go inside, I thought to myself, *"How dare you tell me to go take off my coat! It's not bothering you or anyone else, for that matter!"*

Good thing it was just a thought because if he could have read my mind, I believe he would have killed me.

I grew up in a huge house where we didn't have a whole lot. Although my parents had great jobs, our home was nothing short of a castle. We were a poor, yet close-knit family. Our home had two temperatures during the year: extremely hot or extremely cold. So, during the summer, we stayed outside and, during the winter, we would all huddle in the kitchen over the oven to keep warm.

I was always the "cry baby" of the family (so everyone says). I think I only cried when I got into trouble or whenever we were playing, and I got whooped or blamed for something I know for a fact I didn't do. My parents were very strict when it came to my little sister, though. She was mommy and daddy's little girl for sure. We could be playing outside or horsing around upstairs in the attic, and if my dad heard her cry for any reason whatsoever, one of us was going to be in some serious trouble…and that was no exaggeration.

Saturday mornings always seemed to be the worst when we were watching cartoons. My little sister had this massive craving for spaghetti and would always grab a dining room chair, sitting right in front of the TV with her bowl — as if no one else was sitting in the living room but her. We would yell, *"Callie, get out from in front of the TV!"* My brothers and I would try not to stir up an early morning commotion because we knew mom would start yelling at the top of her lungs from the top of the staircase. Callie would move her chair over about an inch or two and, by this time, dad would've made his appearance known by walking through the kitchen door to check out the scene, just to see if we were bothering his darling daughter. She had us all in the palm of her hand…and she **KNEW** it. If you were to ask her today, she would, of course, beg to differ.

As a child, I felt like there was a major piece of the puzzle missing in my life. Although I couldn't quite put my finger on it, I never felt like I accomplished much of anything throughout my childhood and teenage years. I feel like I only scratched the surface at everything I put my hands to. In other words, I would start projects but never finished them. I didn't know how to stay focused half the time. Back then, I guess you could equate that as having a learning disability. Not to mention, I had a significant stuttering problem, which made things a lot more difficult for me as well.

I would work on a project, and my mind would draw a complete blank. I literally could not comprehend what was in front of me, no matter how much I tried. I would sit in class completely lost and ashamed to speak up for fear of being ridiculed by my classmates or reprimanded by the teacher. I hated school with a passion! I hated the very thought of the breakfast bell ringing to let the students know that the day was starting. I knew it was going to be another difficult day of learning for me.

The teacher would often provide the students with small incentives for those who could solve the most math problems on the flashcards or win the Spelling Bee or earn the most (star) points for class participation. I never mastered any of those. So, of course, I dreaded being called on—much like in Sunday School. I knew it would be a matter of time before the teacher would call me out into the hallway to have a private conversation with me about my grades. She would quietly inform me that I was going to repeat the same grade and that she would be notifying my parents—which was the wrong thing to do! My parents were **NOT** having it.

When we arrived home from school, it was our job to be in those books by the time my parents walked in the door from work. Sometimes, dad would play the mediator and drill us on our schoolwork to give my older sister a break so that she could get her own homework done. She was the "A" honor roll student of the bunch, so she could afford to go across the street to her best friend's house to get away if she wanted to.

Still, with all the efforts to help me learn, I ended up repeating the 5th grade. My parents worked a lot, and most of my brothers and sisters were either married or in relationships. Nevertheless, we remained close. I just wanted to live my life as a normal kid. I hated the thought of having to prove myself in everything to be socially accepted.

The Other Side of Me

I attended Catholic school shortly after that. My parents thought that by removing me from the public-school system, I would have a chance of getting a better education. In their sincere efforts, I still proved to be a slow learner. I couldn't comprehend much of what was being taught in the classroom, so I decided to channel all of my attention on the girls and some of the attractive female teachers every chance I got. I knew absolutely nothing about having hormonal feelings; I only knew something was intriguing about women.

If I described my life in only two words, they would be **weird** and **complicated**.

Chapter Two

Life Lessons to Live By

Our parents provided for us the best way they knew how. The love that they had for their children was like no other. We may not have had much, but we had love for each other — and that was something my parents made sure to instill in us.

The church was very much a part of our upbringing. Whenever our parents were having a deep conversation, and we were anywhere in the room, mom would always channel it towards us by saying, *"Just keep living. You may not understand it now, but you will one day when we're dead and gone!"*

In virtually every conversation we ever had, our parents' motto was, *"You better stay in school and get all the education you can because it's a 'dog-eat-dog' world out there. Your dad and I won't be around forever to tell you this."* As much as I hated hearing them recite that motto like a broken record, it has carried more weight in my endeavors today than it did almost 30 years ago.

Somehow, I knew there was something different about me; I just didn't know in what way. I didn't know how to feel or what to feel because my emotions were skyrocketing out of control and my thoughts were all discombobulated.

The Other Side of Me

"I became afraid of what I didn't understand – life."

I tried fitting in with all the other kids by learning the latest dances, dressing according to what the "hip" fashions were, and even spoke their street lingo. In my attempt to be socially accepted, I soon learned I "wasn't light-skinned enough" to fit in. I wasn't the school's star quarterback or the teacher's pet. On top of it all, my speech impediment didn't win me any phone numbers or dates to the school dance. I was just a lost cause.

What in the world was I good for if I was faced with all of these daily challenges?

Although I was no break-dancer, I was a huge Michael Jackson fan. I spent most of my time in the mirror trying to mimic his iconic moves. I wouldn't have called myself a 'work in progress'; I was a 'hot mess in progress'! I thought I was talented enough to become a huge Mega Star, though. As such, I found myself constantly in practice mode. I often wondered what it would be like to try my hand at acting and music, so I started writing poetry and playing the drums and keyboards in our family.

Unfortunately, I didn't possess the confidence that others around me had. I was this silly, timid guy who people thought was funny. I accepted that title and moved on. The idea of putting my humorous side on film was so out in left field to me. Even though I believed I could do great things, I didn't know how to perfect any of them.

Have you ever found yourself asking God why life is so hard for you or why you can't seem to figure out who you are and what role you are to play in this life? The Bible has always been tough for me to read because I honestly didn't understand its purpose in my life. I didn't comprehend the *"this, thou, and thus"* of the Bible, although I am not knocking it under any circumstance. I am merely stating what it was like for me growing up as a kid. We went to church every Sunday, yet I left out of there knowing very little about God because I couldn't articulate nor interpret the Word at that time. Even now, it's sometimes difficult for me to understand.

My dad was a man of very few words, but when he spoke, he would have everyone in the room laughing hysterically. He was a no-nonsense kind of guy who would tell you like it was—whether you liked it or not. Whenever some of my older brothers brought girls to the house, they would introduce them to our parents. Dad wouldn't ask them much of anything right away because his body language did the talking for him. We could always tell when he liked or disliked a girl by one of two ways:

1) He would welcome them with a warm smile; or
2) He would wait until they left and then ask his six famous questions:
    a. *"Who's that ugly girl you brought here?"*
    b. *"Where did you find that 'hood rat'?"*
    c. *"How many yaps [kids] does she have?"*
    d. *"How many baby-daddies does she have?"*
    e. *"How many of them are yours?"*

The Other Side of Me

    f. *"How many of them does she want you to buy pampers for and play daddy to?"*

Of course, he would be so kind as to offer the girls a plate of food to eat before leaving.

My parents would sit in the living room snickering and mumbling while giving their 2-cent feedback. Sometimes, they showed us absolutely no mercy. Other times, they would encourage us just to be careful of who we dated. My parents were cool in that area.

Dad and mom worked very hard to provide for us. They owned several properties and spent a considerable amount of time renovating them. Dad worked at the U.S. Steel Reduction Company, and mom worked for Goodyear. Every time we saw the Goodyear Blimp in the sky, we would automatically assume mom was inside of it looking down on us, waving and smiling.

We always knew when dad was home from work by the sound of his old truck. We also recognized the sound of the jingling of his keys rattling as he approached the back door. Like clockwork, he would retire to the basement where we could hear him piddling around and moving things from one end of the basement to the other. His hobby was fixing up the old cars that sat in the backyard. After a while, dad would call it a day, come up from the basement, and slip some sweet potatoes into the oven for us. While waiting for the sweet potatoes to finish cooking, he would get a chair, place it in front of the oven, and fall asleep with his feet on top of the oven door.

Often, we couldn't tell the difference between the smell of his feet and the potatoes. We would all wait patiently for the food to cook and then wake him when we knew they were done.

Those were, indeed, some good times...

When our parents weren't home, my older sister would look after us. She would prepare dinner and help us with our homework. In exchange for her hard work, she would send Kenneth, Neiko, and myself to the store to get candy for her. Her list of items would always seem like a grocery list. She always managed to keep a smile on our little faces by meeting our sweet tooth's needs and giving us the change from our trip in honor of our good deed. There was never a dull moment in our household when our parents weren't home.

Rainy days, on the other hand, were a different story. Kenneth and I would stand in the window, sucking on our drooling thumbs while calling out for our mom to come home (as if she could hear our cries). We would also go to the attic to play 'house.' Kenneth somehow would always have the best home renovations. I, on the other hand, had to scrounge up what I could find to make my little pad suitable for visitation.

My grandfather, Merle, would often visit and, on many occasions, it would be 95 degrees outside when he came. No matter what the temperature was, when he arrived, we knew to go outside because that meant grown folk were talking and we weren't a part of the conversation. It seemed like it took him at least 20 minutes to park his car because he was one who never liked anyone messing with or driving his car. Still, we could rest assured that he would say someone had been 'monkeying' with his car overnight. My mom would try hard to be sympathetic and keep a smile on her face to reassure grandpa that everything was going to be okay. Grandpa had the cleanest green 1972 Chevy Impala in our neighborhood. To my knowledge, he never allowed his car to get dirty. One could literally eat off his car's floors and seats because he never allowed anyone to ride in his car. He rarely took anyone anywhere, unless it was our mom.

Grandpa would get out of his car and yell, *"Hey, kids! How y'all doing?"* God rest his soul…he never could get any of our names right. He would always call us whatever name came to mind. After a while, we learned to go along with whatever name he came up with — and we stuck to it for that visit because we knew that the following week, we would adopt some other random name. Another fond memory is how he never forgot to give us all a quarter before making his way into the house. He would always tell us that he had soda and donuts at his house for us. Even though we knew the donuts were stale and the soda was flat, we would get so excited nonetheless. It was just the mere fact that he loved us just that much to keep sweets around for us that kept joy in our hearts.

Our grandfather's home was immaculate and always quiet. He was also a tidy dresser. I can't say that I ever recall seeing him eat or cook a meal in his home because everything always seemed to be in perfect order. There was very little in his apartment, and when we visited him, we would sit on the sofa as he sat in his favorite dinette chair and vented about random topics. All the while, we tried scarfing down those dry powdered donuts he saved for us. He was truly the best grandfather anyone could ever have.

When grandpa outgrew his apartment, he moved to another complex that did not require him to climb stairs. Oddly enough, his new place was much smaller than the one he moved out of—and it was secluded. He was closer to the local grocery store and a car wash. A bonus was that the area seemed to have less drama (that appeared to be all he cared about).

Shortly after his relocation, the visits came to a halt because of the distance in which we lived. We couldn't walk across town to grandpa's house; mom and dad weren't having it. We soon lost complete contact with him.

As we grew older, my siblings and I would often find ourselves going to the neighborhood's poor kitchen when mom and dad were working, and there wasn't much to eat at home. The food was nothing in comparison to mom's cooking, but it was better than not eating at all.

I must stop right here and say that this is **NOT** about painting a negative picture of my parents. We all know that *"if a man doesn't work, he doesn't eat"*!

Often, we would make syrup, ketchup, mustard, or mayonnaise sandwiches along with a jar of coffee if we got hungry enough. We just knew how to make the best of the situation with what we had. We always loved it when our big brother and his fiancé would visit because it was inevitable: We were going to McDonald's! There was a special kind of joy in knowing that we were going to be rewarded for no reason at all.

My brother and his fiancé were the perfect couple. They knew how to meet our needs at the right time. The older I got, the more I loved her because she was the one who told it like it was. Sometimes, it was a bit much, but she was my 'Big Sis' and could get away with it. I loved it when she and I would peel potatoes and make French fries for everyone. You knew they were good when they hit the hot grease and flames shot up to the kitchen ceiling! Our fries were just as good as McDonald's — if not better. Today, she and I are still known for making the best French fries in the family. I miss her so much. I miss her laughter, jive-talking, and the no-nonsense-ready-to-get-with-you-if-need-be woman. She was stunning, smart, and by far my favorite sister-in-law.

Chapter Three

Getting Through School

Getting through grade school was tough for me. When I was around 7 or 8 years old, my parents discovered I had a hearing and throat problem. Often, as I watched TV and my parents would call my name, I didn't know they were talking to me or even in the same room for that matter. Ignoring them wasn't something I did on purpose. I wasn't seeking to get some sort of attention, either. I just couldn't explain to everyone why I cried so much from the painful earaches and throat problems. Because of that, my siblings were very protective of me and would try to understand my dilemma, even though they had no idea what was going on with me at the time.

My parents finally realized that maybe I needed to see a doctor. They soon discovered the source of my distress, which resulted in me getting my tonsils and adenoids removed and tubes put in my ears. For a short while, I became the little *"Golden Child"* of the family who could do no wrong. My parents became extremely loving, nurturing, sympathetic, and attentive. I loved them for that and even got to see them more often.

The Other Side of Me

By the time I reached 6th grade, I was just about a lost cause. I had so much trouble keeping up with the teacher in the classroom, that I would get frustrated and afraid that everyone in the room was going to pass me up again. I had never heard the terms "slow-learner" or "ADHD." I remember having the hardest time finding the pages numbers in a textbook. I would sit there for an hour and never raise my hand to let my teacher know because I feared I would be looked upon as the 'classroom dummy.'

I despised math and science and never liked being called to the blackboard to do any type of problem-solving or analogy. I was utterly clueless as to what was going on, and I hated myself for whatever "it" was. I also disliked not having the ability to think for myself, leaving me to question, *"How did I get all the way through school and still not know a darn thing?"* School was the most humiliating time of my life. My sister, Pat, helped me a lot by staying up late with me to get my homework done. Sometimes, she would even complete it for me when I fell asleep. By the time school started the next morning, all I would need to do was fill in the blanks. To this day, I owe her my greatest gratitude for her sacrifices.

Why couldn't I be smart like the teacher's pet, Olivia? Or like Steven, the one whose parents dressed him in the finest clothes and ensured his lunch always looked and smelled better than the cafeteria food? He was also the "eye candy" of the classroom. God, I hated when he came to school. I would often wish Steven would get deathly ill or that his parents would move him to another school, just so he would stop racking up all the girls with his high-yellow skin, sandy-brown curly hair, neatly-creased "bougie" outfits, and having all the correct answers to the teacher's questions. That kid was a real thorn in my side.

I hated when we received the little paper grade cards (progress reports) throughout the year that let the parents know how their child was doing in school. My twin brother and I pretty much already knew our fate and the consequences that would come as a result. Neiko and Pat, on the other hand, were excelling in every area of their academics. My older sister, Bettye—mom's "tell-all person"—would be the bearer of the bad news and gave our parents the "411". By the end of the day, all my siblings would know that my brother and I failed—or at least one of us had.

Chapter Four

My First Exposure to Pornography

I remember my first encounter with porn. I was 12 years old and walking down an alley near my house on my way home from school. I saw some dirty magazines spread alongside an old garage with exposed body parts I had never seen up close before. Of course, I knew the difference between male and female body parts, but I had never seen adults portrayed like those in the magazines. My first thoughts were, *"How disgusting that someone would drop these porn magazines in an alley and just leave them!"* The very thought of listening to my brothers as they sweet-talked to their girlfriends on the phone at night was creepy enough, but it wasn't to this extent. I walked away from the magazine and went about my way.

As I was walking home from school the following day, I noticed the same magazines were still in the same place as they were the day before. I tried walking past them, but a beautiful woman who was intriguing to me from head to toe caught my eye. Never had I seen a woman so beautiful up close and personal. I quickly gathered up as many of the magazines my little hands could carry and secretly hid them away in the back of my bedroom closet when I arrived home.

Keith Hughes

I recall gobbling down my food at dinner that night.

I was hungry for **flesh**, not for natural food.

My little heart and mind were set on getting to know who the grown woman was in those pictures that had captivated my mind. Somehow, I managed to break free from the dinner table. I ran upstairs to my dark cave of lust and barricaded my bedroom door with heavy objects. I turned on the night light and listened carefully to the sounds outside of my door to make sure the coast was clear.

I grabbed the magazine where I saw the luscious beauty. There she was—in all her glory for me to see. I felt my chest pounding heavily and my mouth salivating as I viewed what I would equate to a large piece of chocolate cake. As I began quietly thumbing through the pages with both eyes adoring all of that glistening, golden flesh and my ears posted to the door as my security, I started feeling things inside of me I never thought existed.

As time progressed, I found myself daydreaming in school about being with the women in the magazines, although I wouldn't have known what to do with them (I had yet to learn all about how the male body part worked). I soon found myself desiring to have even more porn magazines. Whoever had the stash knew just where to leave the material because I could always find more flesh-gratifying magazines in that same alley.

The day I had my first climax was memorable, indeed. My flesh had kicked into overdrive. The experience was scary at first because I had no idea what was happening to me. I didn't know what to think of it because my father had yet to share with me the intricate details of "the birds and the bees."

As the days went by, thoughts of masturbation would enter my mind at the most inopportune moments; in school, at home around family members or just a random thought that popped up in my mind. Instantly, I would get the urge to satisfy my thirst to feed my flesh what it wanted. By the age of 14, my flesh had completely taken over. It was as if it was controlling me, telling me when it wanted to be fed. I had no control or say-so over my feelings because I didn't know how to control them. This lustful demon had become a part of my life, my character, and almost my god because I had become a submissive slave to the desire. It had become *"The Other Side of Me."*

The more I fought my flesh, the more it seemed unsatisfied. I began to find beauty in a woman's feet. As strange as that may sound, my mind and body had gone on a rollercoaster ride of its own — one that seemed like it was never going to end. I started craving the mere thought of touching women's feet because of its connection to the body. For the woman who took excellent care of her nails and feet, she was to be commended for enhancing her beauty.

Next came the obsession with porn websites. The vast availability of them had completely overtaken me. It had become increasingly difficult for me to watch movies with any type of sexual connotation. My spirit-man would tell me I don't need to commit a sinful act, yet my natural man would say,

"Too late! You've already thought about it. You might as well do it and get it over with!" Instantly, my mind would compute the latter is something gratifying, causing me to become sexually aroused. Ultimately, my flesh would win every time because it had taken full control of my mind.

That demonic spirit that threw me into a pit of pure darkness was a part of my life for 38 ½ long years.

Why did I experience those things at such an early age? What did it mean? What was I supposed to gain or learn from it? I wanted to tell someone but, in my mind, I thought it would be the biggest mistake of my life—not to mention the biggest butt whooping of my life. I needed to ask someone if what I was going through was normal. Did I do something that bad to bring shame and disgrace upon myself? I didn't want to be ridiculed or made fun of, so instead of speaking out about it, I decided to put on a mask of deception—the one that would become the identity of **"The Other Side of Me."**

So, there I was as a 14-year-old kid in high school with serious flesh "issues" and thoughts that spiraled fully out of control. Sure, I was raised in the church, but I didn't know how to channel those feelings in the right direction. I hadn't received instruction on how to go to God in prayer for myself. I wouldn't know what to say to Him anyway. All I knew was that I had gotten caught up in something I couldn't seem to break away from.

So many of our children today suffer from a lot of these same issues or worse because of the negative influences around them either from the home front, social media, the classroom bully, or struggling to be something or like someone they're not in hopes of gaining some sort of recognition or acceptance. Often, they are led onto the path of taking their own life along with others, or they spend an enormous amount of time behind prison walls.

If you asked a parent how their child got to that place in their life, many of the responses would likely go a little something like this: *"My Joey/Samantha was a quiet, vibrant child who loved life. Sure he/she started acting out in school and became withdrawn after their father and I divorced."* What child wouldn't?

Enter in the parent's denial that says:

"Oh, no. **MY** *child would* **NEVER** *bring harm to anyone. He is a gentle giant. He had to be pushed over the edge to cause him to do those things."*

"Hey, listen: I know **MY** *child. They would* **NEVER** *do those things they're being accused of doing. That doesn't sound anything like* **MY** *child."*

"The school and the court system simply don't like **MY** *child. They all have it out for him. They want to see my baby fail."*

"If only others would try to understand that he/she has fallen on hard times and never quite recovered, they wouldn't be so judgmental. They would show compassion and see that **MY** *child has a good heart and means well."*

*"So what if he's 35 years old and still living in my basement? Does that make me an enabler? A bad mother? He's still **MY** baby!"* (Some mothers do and say that often.)

Whether you realize it or not, many of you have heard those excuses a million times over. In some cases, you have even washed your hands of it and said, *"He/She will never change"* or *"He/She will just have to work it out some way, somehow because we understand that some things don't always 'just happen' on a humbug."* Often, we bring a lot of things upon ourselves and expect someone to come to our rescue.

It sounds like we're talking about Jesus Christ, huh?

We get ourselves into a predicament without thinking of the consequences, and once things become bad and out of our control, now we want Him to step in and instantly fix the problem without us learning the lesson from it. Yes, God is forgiving, compassionate, and loving, yet He doesn't want us to keep repeating the same cycle. We need to stop putting Satan's signature on our mess, saying *"The devil's always busy!"* when, in fact, we're the ones busy causing the problems!

The truth of the matter is that, like many children, my parents didn't know "me" during my teenage years—not to any fault of their own. I didn't show signs of being in any real trouble; nor did I feel comfortable even talking about my private matters with them. Much like the average kid, I played in the band, did my schoolwork, went to church regularly…and struggled with a strong sex addiction while living at home with my parents. We barely even knew each other because they were either always at work or one of their rental properties working on renovations.

As a result, I got caught up in a 38 ½ year, out of control flesh pool that included drugs, unprotected sex, porn websites, masturbation, loss of countless jobs, infidelity in my first marriage, and an almost sure ticket to the county jail for unpaid child support.

Folks, this was the story of my life. This was, indeed, **"The Other Side of Me!"**

I often reflect and wonder how I made it over…literally!

- Why did God spare my life from drowning and avoiding those car accidents that should have claimed my life on many occasions?
- Why did He spare my life from the heart attack that took my father's life?
- Why did He take my father away from me without us making amends? *(I didn't hate my father; I just didn't know him all that well such as his likes, dislikes, favorite color, his side of the family.)*
- Why did He spare my son's life so many times when many parents' sons and daughters didn't make it? *(By no means do I mean that condescendingly.)*
- Why didn't I have a real relationship with both of my parents?

> Why did my obsession for sex, porn, drugs, a strange foot fetish, marital infidelity, countless job losses, and bad relationships overtake me?

Those (and some other) questions are ones that used to haunt me when I looked back over my life. I didn't play the victim. I didn't hold any strong animosity towards anyone. I became extremely emotional and angry with myself because I thought it was something I had done wrong throughout my life. I held myself in contempt. I didn't know how to forgive myself for all that had taken place in my life. I didn't know that forgiveness was for me first. I didn't know that in marriage, *"in your anger, do not sin."* The Bible instructs us not to let the sun set while we are angry.

My thoughts were, *"Leave me be and give me time to get over whatever it is that we're feuding about. I'll get back to you when I feel like it."* I didn't give two seconds to the thought that my children were being affected by watching their mother and I have disagreements. In my defense, I felt justified in my behavior and less concerned with everyone else's feelings in the house. *"Just do as I say, and we'll get along just fine."*

Here's another truth: At the age of 27, I wasn't ready to be a husband and father. I barely had a job and could barely feed myself. Before that, I was living foul with my ex before we broke off our relationship. I never took the time to recover from that to get myself together. I just plunged right into another relationship, shacked up, got married, and, before I knew it, I had a son on the way.

The Other Side of Me

I was seeking to fill that void in my life at any cost. It didn't matter whose feelings were involved because I needed that emptiness filled with something…someone. I know that may sound insensitive to some of you, but this was truly my reality and outlook on life.

Chapter Five

The Move to Cincinnati

Now, let's quickly recap. I had gone from junior high into high school. I started meeting new friends, dating and trying to get in where I could fit in to be socially accepted. As the year went on, I joined my high school band and made very few friends along the way. While trying to figure out how the whole herd of personalities of hormones and popularity groups clicked, I found myself getting involved with a young lady who seemed rather nice, reserved, very smart…and stuck on herself. Neither of us knew that we would eventually go beyond the boundaries of friendship.

I wasn't all that "easy on the eyes" because girls back then didn't care for the brown-skinned brothers (if you know what I mean). The wavy hair, brush-toting, light-skinned guys with the Jheri Curls, pointed-toe shoes, collar flipped, and embroidered football/basketball jackets were the guys who symbolized that they were of some importance. Yeah, well, I was one of Scott High School's best percussionists in the band. I showed out every chance I got on the field at the games and in the parades for the ladies. All I got, in the end, was, *"Good job, Keith! Keep tearing up those drums!"* **Wow!!!**

The Other Side of Me

High school seemed to pretty much be an extension of grade school. I did just enough to get by to say that I was a graduate. I knew that I wanted a better life for myself, so I decided that after graduation, I would head off to college—no matter what it took. I wanted to get away from my parents' house and go live life to the fullest.

I graduated (late) from high school on June 11, 1987. Two weeks later, I moved to Cincinnati, Ohio with exactly $2.00 in my pocket. That's right—two measly dollars to my name. As we were traveling there, my parents gave me a couple of dollars to put in my pocket and then took me to an old grocery store called 'IGA' to buy a few things for the house that was provided by the college coach. I hadn't confessed to my parents yet that I wasn't sure where I was going to live because I didn't have a direct contact person or any available financial aid. I just knew that I was **NOT** getting back into that car to go back to Toledo.

I finally found Cincinnati Community Technical College. I went inside and spoke with the basketball coach to explain my dilemma. He made me an offer to put me up in one of his campus homes if I found a job and enrolled in the university the beginning of the Fall semester. Although none of my ducks were in a row, that was my ticket out of Toledo. I wasn't going to disappoint him or myself.

Who knew that as I was in the process of getting things in order, I would meet the woman of my dreams? She was sweet, kind, gorgeous, easy on the eyes, and would do anything for anybody. What I loved most about her was that she was smart, beautiful, and came from a Christian family that was full of love. My family loved her like she was their very own. In the three years that we were together, both of our families had given us their blessings for marriage.

Throughout the relationship, I noticed little changes in her behavior. She wanted to spend more time with her best friend, Yvonne, and a couple of our mutual college friends. She told me she felt we were spending way too much time together and that she felt smothered by me. I couldn't agree more. I was at her house so much, her parents offered me a room in their attic! She and I were inseparable then. However, I took the offer with the agreement that I would live upstairs in the attic at night and look for a part-time job to work after class. Meanwhile, her parents would keep tabs on my progress and monitor our relationship to "keep it clean." It was not ideal for them to take in someone who was dating their daughter, but they realized that I moved out of the coach's house and was trying to establish my own.

My girlfriend decided she wanted some time to herself and felt that her other guy friends were of great importance to her. She expected that I respect her desires by giving them their personal space. I knew then that our relationship was coming to an end. We had heated arguments, she stayed out extremely late, and many of my calls went unanswered. I attended her family church and, boy, was it difficult seeing her every Sunday.

I decided I had done just about enough, chose to call it quits, and moved out. Shortly after we broke up, I joined The Testament Worship Center Ministries (TWC) and became a part of the praise and worship team and the pastor's armor bearer. TWC was a non-denominational ministry headed by Pastors Earnest and Tina Duncan. I joined because of the Word of God that was being taught and preached. I loved the people and what the church stood for. I wanted a church family that I could become a part of and grow in. It was the best time of my life, and I was learning how to be effective in ministry and every other area of my life.

Chapter Six

The Birth of My Son and the Music Business

Prior to joining TWC, I did the unthinkable once again. Having not learned from the first, second, third, fourth, and fifth time that it is not right to hop from one woman to the next, I met a young lady with two small daughters. A mutual friend introduced us. I went to dinner at her house that afternoon after church, and within months, we started seeing each other. We tried to keep our friendship as plutonic as possible but realized that everyone could see that we were, indeed, "friends with benefits." So, we decided to make it official. *(That's not to glorify the sin itself; I'm just acknowledging that I was living in sin and this was the truth of the matter.)*

Before our committed relationship, my ex-wife shared with me that her youngest daughter had Sickle Cell Anemia— "a group of disorders that cause red blood cells to become misshapen and breakdown." It is an inherited form of anemia— a condition in which there aren't enough healthy red blood cells to carry adequate oxygen throughout the body. With Sickle Cell Anemia, the red blood cells become rigid and sticky with the shape of sickles or crescent moons. It is a rare disease, with fewer than 200,000 cases per year.

- Treatment can help, but the condition can't be cured.
- Sickle Cell Anemia requires a medical diagnosis.
- Lab tests or imaging is always required.
- It is a chronic condition and can last for years or be lifelong.

My ex-wife gave me the opportunity to think about whether or not I wanted to be in a relationship with her, knowing the status of her daughters and filling the role as a father figure in their lives. I had no life manual or blueprint on how to be a father. I didn't know the first thing about taking care of a sick child. What was I to do?

I commend my ex-wife for the extraordinary job she has done all these years with Briana, Brittany, Adrian, and Christian. Both girls have grown into beautiful, bright women and have gorgeous children of their own. The boys aren't doing too bad themselves, either.

So, after much consideration, we got married and, within a year and a half, she announced that we were going to have a child. I was devastated, confused, happy, and crying all at the same time because I was unsure how I felt about bringing a child into this world when I was already dealing with two other girls and trying to pursue a music career in R&B. That was the life I wanted. I wanted to hit the big stage and see my name in bright lights. I wanted to perform across the world. I felt like I was just as good as the other musical greats out there, so I, too, like many others, wanted a piece of the R&B world.

Keith Hughes

I jumped from R&B to Contemporary Gospel because I had a love for both. I couldn't decide which of the two made me the happiest. I just knew there was something awesome about the rhythm and beat that each had to offer, and found myself entangled in both. I talked to other artists around Cincinnati that I knew could connect me to some of the biggest names in the music business. That was the direction I wanted to head.

Yes, I was straddling the fence big time. I wanted my cake and eat it, too. I believed I could make an impact with either choice.

The 1990s were filled with some of the greatest moments of my life. I started developing a love for writing R&B, Contemporary Gospel music, plays, love poems, motivational skits for colleges, middle schools, and churches in parts of the Ohio-Kentucky area, and modeling in fashion shows. I did go on to write two major play productions called *"Daddy, Please Don't"* and *"Mama's Lil' Angel."* I also played a soldier in the worldwide hit opera play production, *"Aida,"* with the legendary American operatic mezzo-soprano signer, Denyce Graves.

Shortly after that, I performed several times in the Cincinnati Midwest Regional Black Family Reunion — one of Cincinnati's largest family-focused events. I auditioned alongside my ex-wife where we both played extras in the 2000 film *"Traffic"* with actors Michael Douglas, Catherine Zeta-Jones, Don Cheadle, and Dennis Quaid…just to name a few. After *"Traffic,"* I did a live audition for "WB" shows on the official site of the CW Network, and was a guest motivational speaker for the *"Step Up Toledo, Inc."* broadcast production in Holland, Ohio.

My final opportunity to the "bliss of stardom" came when I went into the studio to record a single for a small independent upcoming record label called Vintone Records out of Atlanta, Georgia. The producers (names that I care not to mention) were looking for hot, new, upcoming Cincinnati artists who were making a name for themselves. I was looking to get out of doing housekeeping for a living, so it was a win-win for everyone...or so I thought.

A good friend of mine who was working in the same hotel as me wanted to introduce me to some of his up and coming Atlanta record producers, as they asked me to sing for them. The rest is history. Over time, we all developed a bond-like brotherhood. We were sure we were well on our way to the top. The whole music vibe was good, performance dates were booked, and I was sharing the studio while collaborating and singing hooks with some of the greatest artists and musicians Cincinnati had to offer. We all celebrated what we thought was going to be the "fruits of our labor."

We had finally hit the big-time—so we thought! Then, the inevitable happened. Some of the artists started complaining about their music not getting enough studio time for publishing rights issues and air-play time. The producers were trying to push some of the other artists out of the nest by giving them under-the-table signing bonuses and autograph signing opportunities—without the other artists' knowledge.

I had collaborated with a well-known and established starving rap artist who was getting ready to perform at the Black Family Reunion Summerfest. I was the featured artist on one of his songs. The day we were scheduled to perform, I showed up at the back of the stage just as the host was announcing our names, and the bodyguards would not allow me backstage. We ended up in a heated argument. Somehow, there had been a private meeting between the rap artist and the producers wherein they cut me out of the deal because the artist felt I would be taking bread from his table—but we're "brothers," remember?

There was no meeting with me, the rapper, nor the producers before that show. There were no phone conversations days in advance to let me know those changes were being made. I was told to just *"trust what was happening and that things were being ironed out as we speak."* In fact, the rapper wouldn't even talk to me or return any of my phone calls. In the end, I left with a burnt CD copy of the collaborative piece that we did in the studio…and regrets.

The biggest letdown was when I found myself signing a five-year contract that stated in the 'fine print clause' I was *"not able to sing, sign, or perform with any other record label or major recording artist without being released by my current label."* I was stuck. To add insult to injury, my music producer went to prison on a 10-year bid for a major drug bust. I was devastated, angry, confused, felt led on, and felt like all our hopes and dreams of becoming successful artists were built on one big lie and then thrown back in our faces.

The Other Side of Me

As the days, weeks, and months went by, I found myself isolated and extremely disappointed in myself because I didn't learn anything about the music business. I just wanted to sing! I wanted the big stage and lights, but I didn't want the homework that went along with it. So, in hindsight, I got what I deserved because I wasn't disciplined enough to learn and perfect the craft that God had blessed me with.

I knew absolutely nothing about contracts, receiving residual income, copyrights, and joint-collaborative arts. I was clueless about the game, and everyone knew it. My gig was finally up. I tried to blame everyone else around me as to why things had happened the way they did. I gave every excuse I could to convince those around me that I had been victimized. Some bought it. Others saw straight through me, calling it "the nature of the game."

The most disturbing thing about all this was that the producers and management team seemed to have no remorse for the pain and damage they caused. They treated it as if it had never even happened, and that was disturbing—to say the least.

From that point on, I stopped performing for a while because I couldn't trust anyone. I was done. I threw in the towel and hung up the mic. I closed the stage curtains and turned out the lights. My life was over. As the saying goes, *"All that glitters isn't gold"* — especially when it comes to contracts.

I decided it was time to go back home to Cincinnati and find a job doing something—anything—to keep me occupied until I found out what the next phase was for my life. On many occasions, I was asked to sing at church and weddings. I graciously declined. I made it crystal clear that I would not be dealt a lousy hand ever again. I didn't care if the President of the United States had asked me to perform. Even he would have gotten declined. That's just how deplorable this thing was.

It took me about two to three years to come back around, even though I was still in that cold, unforgiving, bitter stage with the whole record label ordeal. I passionately and justifiably held onto my grudge because anyone with my dreams and aspirations would have been able to sympathize with what I was going through…again, or so I thought!

The adage goes, *"Fool me once, shame on you; fool me twice, shame on me."* That means you should learn from your mistakes and not allow people to take advantage of you repeatedly. The Bible tells us to pray for those who spitefully use us.

"But I say to you, love your enemies, bless those who curse you, do good to those who hate you, and pray for those who spitefully use you and persecute you."
(Matthew 5:44)

The sole purpose in us doing those things is so that our prayers for them would be deliverance from the evil that has been their curse, which is in our power. In praying, we are drawing near to the mind of God and asking that our wills may be as His.

The Other Side of Me

The truth of the matter is that forgiveness can be hard. Of course, that's not to say it can't be done. We all know it can be done. However, the hurt and pain are sometimes still there as a reminder of the traumatic event we endured. On the flipside of that, we serve a mighty God who knows all about our pains and struggles. He is the one who's able to heal you and bring you out of anger, depression, fear, and anxiety. Therefore, prayer is vital in our situations.

So, in doing this, we must learn how to:

1. Stop throwing in the towel or quit in defeat.
2. Stay the course. Keep running to the end of the race or contest.
3. Endure, especially without giving in.
4. Suffer. Wait it out. Wait on God.
5. Understand that your task is a process that you must go through to see the result.
6. *"The race is not given to the swift nor the strong, but the one who endures until the end"* (Ecclesiastes 9:11).

Ecclesiastes 3:3 tells us, *"To everything, there is a season and a time to every purpose under the Heaven."*

As I began to try to find my niche in life, I realized I was gifted in a lot of things but was still asking God for direction as to how to use them. I hadn't perfected any of them, so to me, they were "limited gifts" (if that makes any sense). In other words, I only learned how to play in the key of 'C.' That's why I never volunteered to play the organ or piano for a church.

Although drums are my first love, I never learned the foundational rudiments of any great jazz percussionists to classify myself as one of the greats. However, I can play enough to carry a service. I know how to sing, but it was always the furthest thing from my mind because I personally think I do alright, but not to the point where I'm selling out the Taj Mahal. By no means am I doubting my abilities. I believe I can still learn a lot from watching others or investing in a teacher. However, I'm just saying that I've never really pursued a music instructor simply because my ability to stay focused wasn't there.

Once back in Cincinnati, I was sure about the direction in which I was headed. I made the conscious decision that Contemporary Gospel was where my heart was, and nothing was going to change that. That style of music felt safer and obtainable. I'd decided I was tired of going back and forth with the record labels and that whatever **GOD** had for me was going to be for me.

I returned to TWC and got back on the praise and worship team. For the most part, I chose to stay behind the scenes. Things seemed to work out fine, and I wasn't forced into being at the forefront of the church. I was content with attending church, contributing to the service, and immediately going home afterward.

Much to my surprise, I soon came face-to-face with another recording offer from a gentleman who had visited our church on several occasions. He was dating one of the members named Chloe. Chloe was an amazing, anointed sister who loved God and was a real asset to the ministry. I supported her in just about anything she put her hands to because I knew that whatever she touched was blessed. I didn't know how to say no to her when she told me she loved my singing and had someone she wanted me to meet. Instantly, I thought, *"Oh, my God! Here we go again. Another fly-by-night music producer is looking to get his feet wet with some fresh, local talent. I don't need this."* But because it was Chloe, I couldn't say no to her. So, I agreed to meet with him at his studio.

When I arrived at his home studio, we sat and talked for a while. He told me that he liked my singing and musical abilities—and then asked me if I'd consider singing a couple of bars and hooks on a project he had been working on. Me—being the "go-to person" that I am—agreed to do it. Soon after, we were recording music to present to a couple of record labels in Nashville, Tennessee. My wife had agreed to me doing this after telling me that it just may be the big break I had been waiting for.

So, I decided I'd give it another try. As we were working on my project, the producer introduced me to a gospel rapper who was also trying to make a name for himself in the gospel music industry. It was the producer's idea to have us collaborate on each other's projects to demonstrate our diversity (he wanted to hit all corners of the music genre—ones I wasn't too fond of from the start).

The gospel rapper and I worked tirelessly on one another's projects, but no bookings were being made. The music was getting copywritten, but we weren't receiving even the smallest of a signing bonus. Next thing we knew, the producer says, *"I believe we would be more marketable if we put out Keith's single first featuring 'the rap artist' to get the record labels to buy in."* I could see the frustration in the other artist's eyes, causing me to instantly recall all that I had originally come out of. That was the main reason why I didn't want to revisit this painful and discouraging place again.

I thought I had learned my lesson the hard way. Apparently, it wasn't hard enough.

The time came for us to take the trip to Nashville to try and land a deal and boy, oh boy, was the rap artist furious! You could hear a pin drop in the car, as the tension was so intense. Why were we taking this trip with unresolved issues? Why were we traveling the highways to Nashville when one artist was all in but not the other? Why was this trip necessary at that moment when there was bitter jealousy and strife from the start? The Bible describes this kind of behavior as being in a quarrel, struggle, or clashing disagreement with someone. We **ALL** know that God is not the author of confusion!

There was strife in the Old Testament when Abraham and Lot's herd grew large. The conflict wasn't between Abraham and Lot; rather, *"there was strife between the herdsmen of Abram's livestock and the herdsmen of Lot's livestock. At that time, the Canaanites and the Perizzites were dwelling in the land"* (Genesis 13:7). So, in this instance, strife was a competition between the two herdsmen over the best grazing land for their livestock.

The Other Side of Me

Abraham saw the strife and said, *"Let there be no strife between you and me, and between your herdsmen and my herdsmen, for we are kinsmen"* (Genesis 13:8). Abraham graciously gave Lot the choice of which land to use for his livestock, thereby diffusing the strife between the two men's herdsmen in a very generous and liberal way.

In applying the same biblical concept to the situation with the rap artist to keep down the confusion, we came to some common ground and decided that the rapper's project would be the one we'd try to sell to the record execs first.

When we finally arrived and met with the team of execs, they listened to our music and, after careful consideration, decided that they were going to use my single as a debut sign-on and marketing strategy. That, of course, did not sit well with the rapper. He felt he had been betrayed and stabbed in the back by both the producer and me, although the execs' decision was no fault of ours. They tried to put it delicately that my project had a much stronger message and that they were willing to help him build on his project while collaborating with me on my first single debut. The other artist's level of anger rose even more.

As we sat in the conference room, he told the record execs that he would decline the offer they had placed on the table. I thought to myself, *"A record deal is what we've been working so hard for with all our blood, sweat, and tears! We drove all the way from Cincinnati to Nashville to get a recording contract deal, only to be turned down because of a rapper who couldn't stand being* told he needed to work on his craft. **What a load of crap!**" Now, I was beyond furious!

Although they didn't have to, the execs gave us an extra few minutes to got out into the hall to further discuss their offer. After about a five to ten-minute deliberation, we returned to the office where my produced formally declined their offer. It was the most humiliating experience I had endured to date. It was at that very moment that I (once again) felt betrayed, used, and done with the whole music industry. I walked out of there wishing I could take another form of transportation home because I never wanted to see either of those guys again.

My life had taken blow after blow. My heart had no more compassion for foolishness and letdowns.

The return trip home was a long one. I didn't even bother calling my wife to let her know I would be coming home empty-handed. There wasn't going to be a celebration—just a couple of days to rest and refused all phone calls. In my heart, I hated that I had allowed myself to succumb to what I call "trickery." I knew on the way home that I was going to cut ties with both of those men and, as we approached my street, I asked to be let out of the car.

What was I going to say to my son? How was I going to tell my wife and children that we were going to have to continue hanging in there and hope for the best? How was I going to survive the backlash of criticism from loved ones, friends, and the interrogating questions that led to this major setback?

The Other Side of Me

I walked toward my home on what seemed to be the longest street in Cincinnati that day. Once there, I explained to my wife and children that I had once again embarked upon another failed starstruck adventure.

To this day, my son still calls me with questions about why I didn't make it in the music industry and why I haven't revisited my old play productions or cut an album. The truth of the matter is that I didn't stop operating in my gifts and talents; I just needed a break from the world of music and no longer allowed myself to get entangled with all the "glitter hype" of the music industry and what it had to offer. I often tell my son that I made the conscious decision to return home, go to work, and be a father (the reality of it all was that I was, in fact, needed at home to be a husband and provider, rather than chasing a music career full of empty promises and letdowns). I had enough of my fair share of disappointments.

A couple of weeks after that last disappointing "event," I did some self-evaluating and serious soul-searching to determine all that had gone wrong and what my next move would be. Was it me? Was it them? Was it the record label?

When I say to you that the **TRUTH SHALL SET YOU FREE**, believe me!

After much quiet and alone time, I discovered that the only person to blame was myself. That's right! **MYSELF**. You see, up to this point in my writing, I never told you that I still didn't take the time necessary to discipline myself enough to learn about the music industry, different types of recording contracts, and deals. Hard-headed, right? Well, my mindset was set on cutting records, selling out crowds, living in a mansion…and keeping my pocket phat [loaded].

In all of this, I strongly believe with everything in me that God was looking out for my best interests because He knew we weren't ready for such a significant move. Sure, I could've easily played the 'Blame Game,' but I have no doubt God wanted to use my gifts and me for **HIS** glory. The only way to get my attention was to show me a glimpse of the biggest mistake I would have made at that time in my life by showing me what was to come had I gone through with signing that recording contract. Neither one of us were prepared for the business. That's just the facts!

Today, my son, Adrian, calls me to get my opinion on the music industry, as he is now in the pursuit of fame. My response to him (and to all of you out there who's looking to break into the business) is this (which I say with the sincerest respect):

- Seek God first and ask Him to guide and lead you where **HE** wants you to go.
- Wait for God's response and don't make any sudden moves based on your feelings and notions. Wait on His plan for your life because it may not be the limelight; it may be, instead, reaching the nations).
- Do your homework (read and study the different types of entertainment contracts).
- Learn, study, and perfect your craft.
- Learn about record sales percentages.

- Learn about who's doing what in the music industry (i.e., record labels and artists in every musical genre).
- Listen to and study **ALL** types of music.
- Develop a strong Public Relations (PR) team who can handle your business affairs and will represent your best interests as an artist.
- Don't be "just an artist." Know what's happening at all times with your PR team, the latest entertainment news, and the record labels.
- Learn the nature of the business so that you're never left in the dark.
- Seek legal advice before signing **ANYTHING**!

Once I got settled back into my regular daily lifestyle, I started working in the school system. I did my best to maintain my home life and meet the demands of the church. My wife and I started having little spats and disagreements that weren't really worth the time of day. Those spats grew bigger and bigger, and my trust in her began to fade. I tried to convince myself that I loved her because, at one point, I honestly did.

I even used that old, tired phrase that we can all relate to: *"It's not you; it's me!"* — although I knew **both** of us had issues that needed to be ironed out. I know that all couples go through their ups and downs, and I was convinced that with God's guidance, we could beat the odds. Unfortunately, the odds eventually didn't work in our favor because I started losing trust in her—and I was losing confidence in myself to remain faithful.

I started looking for a way out of the marriage. I began seeing someone else whom I thought understood me better as a person. I lost the interest of my children because I was away from home for hours at a time. I loved them dearly but wanted my freedom to do what I wanted to do and just allow them to make family weekend visits. I no longer wanted to waste any more of their time — let alone mine — because I wasn't interested in being married to their mom.

My son started acting out in school uncontrollably. It seemed like my wife and I were getting phone calls every other day because of his behavior and inability to focus in class. He started getting into trouble constantly and soon, had to be placed on medication, even while we were still dealing with our sick daughter. Our oldest daughter, Brittany, tried to keep everyone in the household intact — and she was only around seven years old at the time, I believe.

Brittany has always been a fighter and outspoken for what she believes in. She simply wasn't one to buy into either one of our excuses: You were either right or wrong. Get it together, own up to your mistake/mess, and move on. I will always love her for that.

My wife found out I was having an affair with another woman and gave me an ultimatum: end the affair or divorce her. Things had gotten so bad in the home that I made the conscious decision to end the marriage. I didn't want to continue hurting her and setting a bad example for our children.

The Other Side of Me

While fighting my marital issues and writing another play production, I received a call from Toledo that my father had passed away from a massive heart attack. That was the icing on the cake. That traumatic news put me clean over the edge. It was one devastating event after the other.

Another part of me felt that my wife and I had married way too soon. Neither of us was really in the position to be a husband or wife. I know you're probably saying, *"Speak for yourself!"* but it's true! I got tired of strange men and women coming to our house at odd hours of the night, the club-hopping, and the disloyalty. So, I moved out, got my own place, still taught at the same school that our children attended, and spent time with the kids on the weekends. I had finally received what I had been asking for: my freedom! In all of this, I was miserable and still couldn't contain my flesh.

Although we were separated, I found that I still couldn't trust my wife, the other woman who professed her love for me, or myself. I was totally dysfunctional in every sense of the word. I would flip-flop backward and forward in my mind, believing I had made a terrible mistake by asking my wife for a divorce. Part of me wanted to return home so bad, but my pride wouldn't let me. Every time I attempted to pick up the phone to call and beg her for forgiveness, my ego would kick in and tell me to "man up and stick to my guns."

I was fighting a losing battle all the way around. I couldn't see God anywhere. Each day was like playing a game of Russian Roulette. I didn't know what each day held to the next. I was just glad to see another day. I didn't know if I was living or dying. My struggle with home life and loneliness would finally lead me to sex, drugs, and alcohol.

I cut ties with the other woman but was still out there just wandering from place to place. I knew that I needed God. I was in a position of "stand still" with no sense of direction and fighting a severe case of anxiety, feeling like I was drowning in sorrow with no hope of recovering. I was ashamed of my children seeing me in this state when I would pick them up from their home or their grandmother's house. It was embarrassing to know that everyone around me could see just how much I had hurt my family.

The relationship with my son started to deteriorate, and I didn't know how to fix it. Eventually, my relationship with the girls would soon follow, and I had no wife to turn to. I had completely lost my family. I found myself alone in my apartment and asking, *"What have I done? How did I get here?"* I had lost everything and everyone who meant anything to me. I felt like I couldn't turn to my immediate family for support and I barely had a friend I could call "my own."

In the end, I found myself alone and tearful because of the dangerous lustful rollercoaster ride my flesh had taken me on. I would not dare rule out the fact that Satan didn't have his fair share of play in all of this, but I will say that I'm one who owns up to my share of mess. Believe me when I say: I know I played a huge factor in this game. I both hated and feared the person I had become—I was my own worst enemy.

The Other Side of Me

I had become so self-destructive that when I went to church, I wore that spirit loudly as I sat at the back of the church and played on the sympathy of the saints while trying to convince them that I was okay. I had no qualms about taunting my tainted behavior. The truth of the matter is that I was embarrassed and, half of the time, ashamed to come to church because I knew many of the people there knew my truth.

Often, we think that we're fooling people when, in fact, they'll allow us to wear ourselves out in our own "pit of lies" before we opt just to come clean.

God was not at all pleased — and neither was I. I knew I needed help but was too ashamed and stubborn to admit it outwardly. The next barrage of questions plagued my soul:

1. Was God removing everything and everyone out of my life because I had lost focus of Him?
2. Was He punishing me for punishing my family with my selfishness and lustful desires?
3. Was I headed for destruction, and this was His way of saving my life and theirs as well?
4. Was I still lashing out and angry with myself at the fact that the music industry had let me down and the recovery was just too much to bear?
5. What was He doing in me? Or what was He trying to do in me?
6. Was I still angry at the fact that my dad had passed away and I didn't get the closure I thought I deserved from those past pains?

Those questions stuck with me for quite some time. I was left to try to figure it all out on my own. I remember praying and asking God to give me some sense of direction as to what He wanted me to do, especially after I had burnt so many bridges. My first thought was to pack up, move back to Toledo, and call it quits (at least the sting of guilt wouldn't have been too bad). In the end, I decided to man up and stay in Cincinnati.

My wife and I started counseling with our church counselor. Our attempts at reconciliation were slow coming, but we went to church every Sunday and back home together as a family. I then joined the praise and worship team once I felt comfortable enough to stand before the congregation. Unfortunately, our attempt to make things work between us just wasn't strong enough to make the marriage last.

When our divorce was finalized, we decided to remain civil for the sake of the children. To this day, she and I have a great relationship as co-parents. She always goes out of her way to ensure my current wife and I are comfortable when we travel to Cincinnati to visit the kids. The divorce taught me that we must wait on God's timing when dating or starting a family.

Often, we don't realize the impact a divorce has on children. We make sudden, rash decisions to "become one" in an unsettled union that God did not ordain in the first place **OR** we get married out of feeling obligated to the other person.

My marriage experience went just like this: We woke up on a Saturday morning and I told her that we were getting married that same day. Of course, she thought I was joking. By that evening, we were joined at the hip.

As I took you on this journey of my life, you could probably tell that I wasn't doing a lot of seeking God's face for a lot of what I went through. I didn't believe He could save my marriage because we were just too far gone to save…so I thought. I want to take the time here, however, to encourage those who may be currently married, considering marriage, or to that single person who's leaning towards the idea of marriage. I strongly suggest that you:

- Take your time. Enjoy the perks of the single life before taking on that kind of serious commitment.
- Make sure you are going after obtainable goals that will set you up for prosperity in the future.
- Make sure God is your center focus with prayer and fasting in all that you set your mind to do.
- Be committed to yourself first. Enjoy **YOU** first.
- Learn who you are in Christ before wanting to learn about someone else.
- You don't need validation from anyone; validate yourself.
- Take yourself out to dinner. Learn how to enjoy time alone.
- Decree and declare that you are the head and not the tail; you are above and not beneath; you are who God says you are.
- Recite to yourself daily, "I can do all things through Christ that strengthens me. I am fearfully and wonderfully made. I am victorious. I will not settle because I don't have to."

- Hold yourself to a higher standard.
- Admit that you messed up. It's now time to get up, dust yourself off, and keep running the race. Why? Because the race is not given to the swift or the strong, but to the one who endures to the end. Therefore, do not wallow in self-pity.
- Right your wrong and move on. (If you have an ought with your brothers, get it right.)
- Don't allow others to define you. Know who you are.
- Know your self-worth.
- Take ownership of your mistakes and learn from them.
- No one can beat you being **YOU**. So, be the best **YOU** that you can be!
- All have sinned and fallen short of the glory of God. No one is perfect except **GOD** Himself.
- Allow yourself time to get to know the other person mentally and spiritually to see whether or not you're even compatible. Just because a person quotes a few scriptures and shouts a couple of *"Hallelujahs"* doesn't qualify them as your 'soulmate.'
- Don't feel like you are missing out on having a "Boo Thang" just because other relationships around you seem to be filled with bliss and fantasy. It's not always what it appears to be and, on the other hand, you don't know what it took for that couple to get to where they are today.
- Contrary to popular belief, everyone does **NOT** like you!
- Don't act thirsty. (I'll leave this one right here. Use your imagination to interpret what I mean.)
- Become the person God intended you to be. Allow Him to bring you that special someone who is spiritual and

can impart something in you and your life — something that's life-changing.
- ➢ Learn how to pray to get the answers you need from God. Discipline is key if you want an answer from Him. He is your lifeline and source. Why not go to the One who is **ALL** and knows **ALL**?

Those are just a few of the things I had to learn the hard way, but I'm glad I did because now, I have a better understanding and outlook on the importance of marriage. Those same tools can and should also apply to my single people and newlyweds out there as well.

My brother and sister, you are worth so much more than what you give yourself credit for. I know I took you down a mountain of events that happened in my old marriage but understand this: Everything I went through wasn't to present you with a pity party in hopes that you would pick a side. Instead, it was set up to let you see how one can lose their focus in God and go down the wrong road when you're **NOT** praying, fasting, and living according to *GOD'S* principles correctly. In the end, I didn't lose; I won because I learned from my mistakes. I paid a heavy price, but I earned a lesson well-learned.

Sometimes, we get set on doing things our own way because we feel it's the best way or we adopt the mindset of believing that we have the situation nipped in the bud — only to make matters worse. God doesn't force His will upon us. He will allow us to make mistakes to get us to see that it is He who we need to fight our battles. We must remember that He knows us better than we know ourselves. He knows what we need before it ever originates as a thought in our mind.

I will say it again: We must learn to trust God at His word and lean on Him and not our own understanding.

> *"'For My thoughts are not your thoughts,
> neither are your ways My ways,' declares the LORD."*
> **(Isaiah 55:8)**

Jesus is not One who throws His weight around. He's not some big bully who goes around picking on the weak. He knows that we need Him to make it. The way I see it is why wouldn't we want to serve Him after He went to Calvary to save a wretch like you and me? He has shown us how much He loves us. What would've happened to humankind if Christ backed out of the crucifixion? It would've defeated His purpose. Simply put, we would be **LOST**!

If we were to study the Garden of Gethsemane at the Mount of Olives in Jerusalem, the Gospel of Mark 14:35 says, *"He [Christ] began to pray that if it were possible, the hour might pass Him by."* In verse 36, Christ says, *"Father, all things are possible for you; remove this cup from Me; yet not what I will, but what You will."* So, as you see, had the plan been stopped, then Jesus wouldn't be God. Had God not decided to come into the Earth as God the Son (incarnate as a man to die as a sacrifice for the forgiveness of sin), he wouldn't have bothered with all of the preliminaries! He would've skipped the whole trip! He would've essentially been looked at as "just a regular, old Joe on a conquest to figure out another way to save mankind." Or who knows? He may have devised an escape plan to shun the Chief Priests and Elders who were coming after Him that night in the Garden.

I said all of that to say this: You can't play house and expect God to bless what He didn't ordain in the first place. We know that God is not the author of confusion. God is the Author of life and is also the Preserver of life. Psalm 16:1 is a prayer that asks, *"Preserve me, O God, for in You I take refuge. I say to the Lord, 'You are my Lord; I have no good apart from You.'"* You can't expect things to work out in your favor when you're living foul. It just doesn't work like that. Again, if you want to obtain the favor of God on your life, then you must believe in Jesus Christ and start living according to His biblical principles. Remember: It's not about you. It's all about Him and His getting the glory out of your life. As saints, it is our job to bring the lost to Christ. It is His job to save them.

I would venture to say that if you haven't already done so, an excellent place to start would be with good, old-fashioned repentance. Acknowledging the fact that you've messed up and need a turnaround in your life is half the battle. John 3:16 says, *"For God so loved the world, that He gave His Only Begotten Son; that whoever believes in Him shall not perish, but have eternal life."*

So, look at the promise that He makes to us when we surrender to His will. He presents us with a "win-win covenant" that cannot be broken. He presents to us eternal life. He knows all about our struggles, heartaches, and pains. That's why He's a heart-fixer. He knew we were going to make a mess of things before we did! That's why He's the mind regulator who helps you get back to your right state of mind. He knows we're hurting, which is why He's our healer. He knows what we stand in need of before we come to Him with our requests. There is nothing new under the sun to Him. Why? Because He created us in His own image. That's why He knows us so well.

My friend, you don't have to stay stagnant and bitter in your effort to forgive. Remember: Forgiveness is for you so that you can move on to greater things in life. Forgiveness doesn't give the attacker a "green card" pass of believing that the pain they caused in your life holds validity. No. There are still consequences and a price that we all must pay. Many people liken that to, *"You do the crime, you do the time!"* So, whatever the ordeal may be, we must remember that *"Vengeance is mine, saith the Lord."* As much as we'd like to play the judge, jury, and executioner, it is **GOD** who has the final say-so in the matter.

If God loved us as much as we'd sinned against him—77 times over and then some—how much more can we forgive those who trespass against us?

Chapter Seven

Reasons God Removes People from Your Life

During my walk with Christ, I've learned that forgiveness is the key to moving on in life because it is linked to our destiny. If we want to see God do great things in our lives, then we must start forgiving people—family and friends—for the petty and troubling things they've done to us. We must ask God to help us with these things. I know it gets hard at times. Our pride asks, *"Why should I always have to be the one to forgive?"* We shouldn't always have to be the one who settles for the "okey-doke" to prove that we're saved, while the other person gets to go around continuously hurting others.

Many times, I have asked God, *"Why do I have to keep taking a slap in the face or be the bigger person? Why do I have to grin and bear it as if I am nothing more than a punching bag or doormat? What am I to gain or learn from this?"*

I've learned that God replaces something painful with something wonderful. He is the source of our blessings and, without the source, there would be no resource! You can always tell when God is getting ready to bless you because He will start to remove people from your life—even ones you depend on the most.

Here's why:

1. Because He wants to make sure that when He brings you out of the storm, you will not have anyone else to praise but Him! God is our source; therefore, when your husband loses his job, but somehow, the checks are still coming in the mail, it's not because of someone's sympathy. That's God's way of saying, *"I GOT YOU!"*
2. Because not everyone who's there for you when you're down wants to see you get back up! No matter how saved and loving you are, there is always going to be someone who dislikes you. The sad part about it is that sometimes, those people are the ones we care most about…our "friends."
3. Because sometimes, our loved ones become more of a distraction than our enemies. This is God's way of keeping us focused. We sometimes place our relationship with God on the back burner without even realizing it. We don't give it our 'all' like we do everything else. That's why we must switch the energy that we currently put into our distraction and refocus it where it's needed: on **HIM**! When God removed people from my life, it was a blessing in disguise. On the flipside of all of this, we sometimes want to remove certain things from our lives that have become a thorn in our side. God may leave it there to remind us that there is a lesson to be learned. What "lesson," you might ask? The answer is this: Whatever that one thing is that may be controlling your life.

The Other Side of Me

It's not that God has plagued you with an unbreakable curse; it's just that there may very well be a lesson in it that He wants you to learn so that you can teach others down the line and help them overcome similar obstacles.

My prayer now is…

"Lord, remove anybody from my life who means me no good, serves me no good purpose, and is not real and loyal.
Bless me with the discernment to recognize them
and give me the strength to let go and not look back."

Looking back and knowing what I know now, I wish I would have understood prayer while I was going through the rocky marriage, the eight-year broken relationship, the battling of my flesh, and the unsettled pain and death of my father — just to name a few. But that's okay because, in the end, I still came out on top. I came out **VICTORIOUS**! And you can, too, my friend! God has not forgotten about you. He cares about you more than you know. His love for you runs deeper than the ocean's floor. His love for you is immeasurable!

So, you see, it is true that He will never put more on us than we can bear. I've learned that faith is the knowledge deep down inside that things will get better. It's taking the next step when you can't see the entire staircase. Simply put, life would fail to have a reason if we didn't have faith. Without faith, we couldn't expect that things would turn out alright for us, no matter what the situation might be.

Today, faith, promise, and God's Word are all I must stand on. So much has happened in our world and indeed, we are living in the last days—the "End Times." There has been a reversal in roles in practically every facet known to man. There is the reverse role of the parents and their children in the home. Our government and city officials have lost their constitutional rights to serve our country with great pride and dignity. Our world, as a whole, has become a 'House of Scandal'! It has become the norm that many people have accepted things as they now are, as long as it doesn't directly affect them, they are okay with it.

There was a time when the church was a 'House of Reverence,' and the White House was a respectable and honorably-held office. These things weigh heavily on my heart because it now seems there is very little or no concern at all that the world we live in can't seem to see how much we need each other to survive. Without God's guidance, how will we continue to stand as a 'global people,' even if we remove the color of one's skin from the equation? We can't even seem to agree on reciting the United States of America's National Anthem anymore without raising the issue of one taking a knee for what he or she believes in.

Our Board of Education has stripped our children of reciting the Pledge of Allegiance, thereby silencing the very mention of God's name. They've done away with cursive handwriting (amongst other things), only to replace them with teachers having strange addictions and lustful relationships with our young boys and girls. We have an enormous high school drop-out rate, bullies pushing their peers over the edge, and babies having babies—yet we say there is a shortage of teachers in the school system. You don't say!

What's interesting enough is that in all of this, the church somehow seems to be in the media's forefront, accused of being the head culprit for a community of dysfunctional sinners and saints. Well, I hate to be the bearer of bad news, but the church wasn't on site when many of those heinous crimes took place, yet the media will somehow drag them through the mud and try to slaughter their name to spread division to a blind people (the world) who needs a Savior. Now, that's not to say those behaviors didn't exist before because the reality is that they have. However, the church should **NOT** be prosecuted and charged for an "act of cruelty" caused by one's own dysfunctional hang-ups and who couldn't cope with the pressures and rules of our society. Because of his or her own selfish hang-ups, we would rather keep living life with a Russian Roulette mentality rather than go to the source who can do anything but fail. His name is Jesus Christ!

Believe it when I tell you that none of those things will matter to God once we are front and center with Him. Folks, we have to see the bigger picture. Luke 21:25 tells us that *"There will be signs in the sun, moon, and stars. On the Earth, nations will be in anguish and perplexity at the roaring and tossing of the sea."* Verses 35 and 36 make it clear that *"…it will come upon all those who live on the face of the Earth. Be always on the watch, and pray that you may be able to escape all that is about to happen and that you may be able to stand before the Son of Man."*

What a privilege and an honor to be able to share with you God's love and the things He's brought me out of, only to give it back to you as words of wisdom, words of encouragement, and hope for a better tomorrow. This book should be your ammunition to go back to the devil's camp and take back what belongs to you. What has God promised you? Has He given you gifts and talents that you have allowed to lie dormant for years for fear of feeling like you're not good enough? Have life's lessons gotten worse as you've tried to make sense of it all, yet for every step you take, it seems like you get knocked back down twice as hard, making it difficult for you to stand on faith?

I know it's hard trying to figure out this thing called "life." What you must understand is that we serve a God who is married to the backslider. Whether you have somehow strayed, are a new babe in Christ, or just curious about who He is, know that He has **NEVER** changed. He's been there all the time—willing, able, and ready to receive you as His own. We change, but He remains the same.

Jeremiah 3:14 says it best:

"'Turn, O backsliding children,' saith the LORD, 'for I am married unto you; and I will take you one of a city, and two of a family, and I will bring you to Zion.'"

In this parable, we are called to repentance. God makes it perfectly clear to us that He has a covenant with us that He is ready to renew. So, that tells us that God has never left our side.

He was right there all the time waiting patiently, yet He never forced His will on us.

My friend, God wants to take you back just the way you are. He is no respecter of person. When He died on the cross for our sins, all excuses were nailed to that cross. He already knew that you and I would fail in our attempts to do right in this life. Again, it doesn't give us a free "sin pass" to continue doing whatever it is that we're doing, but it puts us in place to receive the blessings of God when our hearts and minds are pure, and we have the desire to do what's right. It's called "the desire to do God's will and setting aside our own agendas to abide by His principles."

We must always remember that someone else has it worse off than we do and that every day we have breath in our body, we should take a moment to thank and praise God for His grace and mercy for allowing us to see another day.

Too often, we focus on what we don't have rather than what we already have. Folks, God has blessed us tremendously in our undeserving state, yet we still have not learned how to thank Him for the small things in life. We must remember that it is **HE** who giveth and **HE** who taketh away. He is our source—not man.

We've learned to rely on man to meet our needs when it is **GOD** who gives the increase. It is in our human nature to fall back on what we believe is best suitable for us: using the old "fending for myself method" without depending on anyone else. In our mind, we often believe we have the answers to life's trivial challenges, whether they work to our advantage or not. We sometimes count our blessings and move on or chalk it up as just another day at the office. *"You live another day to try it all over again"*...or maybe not at all. At least we'd know firsthand what we're dealing with.

A world without God? What type of world would we live in if it was Godless? If God wasn't the spearhead of our lives, where would that leave us? Without God, man has a physical presence only. God warned Adam and Eve in the Garden of Eden that on the day they rejected Him, they would *"surely die"* (Genesis 2:17).

Many people wouldn't mind it so much if we didn't have God in our lives because they don't want the backlash of having to answer to a superior being that they cannot physically see. Those same people would rather have us adopt their belief system. According to the online site *Project Inspired*:

- We would be a people without hope.
- Without God, there would be no faith.
- There would be no moral law because people would live their lives without standards. How would they even know what's morally right and wrong?
- No one would be held accountable.
- There would be no meaning to our lives.
- There would be nothing to look forward to.

Christians know that God gave man dominion over the Earth. Genesis 1:26 defines the word 'dominion' as "to rule or have power over." God lets us know that He has sovereign power over His creation and has delegated the authority to humankind to have dominion. David reinforces this truth in Psalm 8:6: *"You made [mankind] rulers over the works of Your hands; You put everything under their feet."*

Mankind was to *"subdue the earth"* (Genesis 1:28). We were to hold a position of command over it. We were placed in a superior role and directed to exercise control over the Earth and all its flora and fauna. Humankind was set up as the ruler of this world. All else was subjugated to him.

So, you see, all authority is of God. We have the power to rule because God gave it to us at the beginning of creation. Therefore, going back to what I was saying earlier about man, he cannot close doors that God has allowed to be opened, nor can he reopened what God has commanded to be closed. You and I have the right to decree and declare in the atmosphere what we want to see God do in our lives. We can seal those things with the covering of our faith, praise, worship, and even with a good 21-day consecrated fast. We consecrate ourselves to draw closer to the Lord to get clear revelation and direction for the next chapter or phase of our lives.

Let's face it: Life is filled with failures and letdowns and, as much as we hate to admit it, we must be realistic and true to ourselves if we ever want to see a change. It really is the way of the world. If we all had a dollar for each of life's failures, we'd be a rich people.

"It's not what you go through, but how you go through it."

You can choose to be victorious, or you can accept defeat. It's your call. However, somewhere in the core of it all is the fine print that says, *"I can do all things through Christ who strengthens me"* (Philippians 4:13). The outcome of your situation is determined by how much positivity (life) you speak to it or how much negativity (death) you speak to it. *"Life and death are in the power of the tongue"* (Proverbs 18:21). Remember: **YOU** can choose what life will hold for you. This is **YOUR** story, **YOUR** life. If all you can ever do is recite the *"What ifs?"* and *"Lord, why me?"* cards, or *"It must not be God's will for me to have 'this or that',"* then the odds may not play out much in your favor because your heart and mind are so smothered by what it is you **DON'T** have versus what God has already blessed you with.

I cannot stress this enough: **YOU HAVE THE ABILITY TO WRITE YOUR OWN STORY.** What will the reader learn and say about you? You should always want to be on the rise, looking for creative ways to improve your life while being a blessing to others in some way. Ultimately, make your primary objective to be pleasing to God and fulfill His principles for your life.

I can promise you no one has ever said life was fair. No one told me that the road would be easy, and I honestly don't believe that God brought **ANY** of us this far to leave us. I want you to see the sincerity of my heart when I consistently emphasize the word "us" because I want you to see that I, too, have been faced with many challenges, letdowns, and disappointments. However, in the end, I know it was all for my good. It was a part of God's plan for my life and for where He is now taking me. On the flipside, I caused a lot of unnecessary roadblocks in my life that clearly could have been avoided had I just taken heed of what God was trying to get through to me in the beginning.

I'm not saying this out of self-pity. Neither am I wallowing in my past failures. I'm simply stating that we all have a choice to live or die and to make good or bad choices. God grants us those opportunities and will not force Himself on us.

Have you taken notice that not once and through all that I've said, I have not brought Satan into the picture? Why? Because I wanted to take on full ownership of the mess **I'VE** caused. That's not to say he didn't play a critical role in a lot of it because I'm sure he did. But as we all know, an idle mind is the devil's playground. I can assure you he gets no "get out of jail free pass" with me.

Folks, every dilemma is not of the devil. I do firmly believe that a lot of it was God's will for my life because it was necessary for me to go that way for me to reach my destiny in Him while keeping in mind that whatever doesn't kill me makes me stronger. Therefore, this makes me victorious! **I WIN!**

Life's setbacks should never be able to win over your destiny. I found out a long time ago that I needed God in my life because I was searching for life's 'happiness' through the eyes of people. I didn't realize that they are just that: people. Man can let us down every time. We let each other down daily—in many instances, on purpose or by pure default. That's why we need a Savior who knows all and is ALL. He not only laid down His life so that we would have eternal life with Him; He also promised us an **EXPECTED** end. We've got to get it rooted deep down in our hearts that man is not our source— **GOD** is. It is not His desire that any of His people perish. The other great thing about our Lord and Savior is that He wants us to be prosperous. Therefore, we are in a win-win situation with God! Our destiny is sealed in Him!

Can you imagine what the endless possibilities would have been for you if you had only given God the opportunity to change your life? The unsolved mysteries that you needed clarity on? Those mountains that seemed unmovable because your faith had been shaken and even seemed stripped, letting doubt to set in? It also took precedence over your ability to believe God for what He had already promised you. It left you secretly wondering if God was ever capable of working out that 'thing' on your behalf, causing you to question Him and call His abilities to the carpet.

Oh, yeah. It's a part of our DNA to believe whatever we choose to believe to have substance and validity, especially if there is a sure benefit to getting something out of it without always having to grind and put work into it. It becomes our mental state to take the easy way out—sometimes referred to as a "hand out" or "getting something for free." That is how many of us live our lives. It's been that way since the beginning of time.

Contrary to what one may say, believe, or think, no one wants to get up and work a 9-5 job every day because we love it. We do it because it's a part of life. It's how we survive. *"A man who doesn't work doesn't eat!"* Right? That's Bible 101 (see 2 Thessalonians 3:10). That's also man's nature. They go hand in hand. Last I checked, **SALVATION** is free! However, you still must work while yet it is the day. Let's not get it twisted!

So, when we get right down to the wire, we are living beneath our privilege because we are a people who still struggle with believing who God is. It is, after all, hard to place trust in a Superior being whom we cannot see, but that's the kicker! The question here is: Whose report will you believe? Let me make it clear that by no means am I stepping on anyone's toes or being blatantly facetious with my comment. I would never do that. I respect my spiritual leaders too much to be called to the carpet about something misconstrued. I need not form a false misunderstanding of my intent. However, we have learned to recite Hebrews 11:1 like it's the National Anthem:

"Now faith is the substance of things hoped for,
the evidence of things not seen."

Therefore, we know that according to James 2:14-26 in the NKJV that *"faith without works is dead."* Faith is an action word. It calls for us to do something. It causes us to put our hands to the plow. James 2:21-24 reads, *"Was not Abraham our father justified by works when he offered Isaac his son on the altar? Do you see that was working together with his works, and by works, faith was made perfect? And the scripture was fulfilled which says, 'Abraham believed God, and it was accounted to him for righteousness.' And he was called the friend of God. You see, then, that a man is justified by works and not by faith only."*

Again, faith and belief go hand in hand. You can't have one without the other. You must work them **BOTH**. If you don't, then how do you expect God to move on your behalf with doubt and unbelief? You cannot move the hand of God operating in that manner. With everything that's going on in our world today, faith is what we'll need to stand on in these *END TIMES*.

I must say that the 1990s were, in fact, the best years of my life because of the birth of my son and all of my accomplishments. I took the good with the bad. I would also add that I wouldn't trade my experiences for anything. They taught me how to endure when times get a little rough and how to trust and love God and my family more. They taught me how to take one breath and one day at a time and to not get so worked up when it seemed like I was about to experience another traumatic rollercoaster ride.

GOD IS IN CONTROL and until we learn that, we will continue to do things our own way. That means we will continue to do things out of order by being impatient.

Another example of that concept would be purchasing a classy vehicle that you know you can't afford. You must decide, *"Do I pay this car note or do I put food on the table?"* — when you should have waited on God in the first place.

The Other Side of Me

I know it's easier said than done a lot of times, but I've learned that patience is truly a virtue. Patience is the ability to wait for something without getting angry or upset. It is a valuable quality in a person. However, the Bible says in Psalm 55:22, *"Cast your burdens upon the Lord, and He will sustain you; He will never allow the righteous to be shaken."*

God is waiting for us to cast all of our cares upon Him. The issue is that when we do give them to Him, we tend to doubt and pick them back up. We don't allow Him to work it out. If we really gave it to Him, then we would know that He is more than able to handle whatever we are facing. The human nature side of us causes us to act out of our feelings by saying, *"If God doesn't hurry up and do it, then I'm going to have to do what I gotta do."* And in that, we can build up a strong sense of fear because we haven't activated or walked in our faith and belief in knowing that God can and will bring us out of the situation that has rocked our world.

So, I found myself going back and forth in my mind, wondering: How do I confront this fear tactic that has bullied me for so long? Well, first I had to face the giant mountain head-on, as I knew that it was time for me to get over it—not go around it, but get **OVER** it. I had to find out what the leading causes of my symptoms were and what proper steps I needed to take to get over those big bullies called 'Mental Fear and Anxiety.' I then had to seek scriptures that spoke to my situation. Remember, though, that **GOD IS IN CONTROL.**

Let's look at the word 'fear' and its usage to provide us with clarity:

FEAR is one of the enemy's most popular weapons that he uses against us. Worry. Anxiety. Fear. All can overwhelm us with a thick cloud of darkness, controlling every move and decision to include:

- A job
- Marriage
- The whereabouts of your children
- Finances
- Past hurts / Relationships
- Your mind

The list goes on and on, but the Word of God says *"So, do not fear, for I am with you; do not be dismayed, for I am your God. I will strengthen you and help you; I will uphold you with My righteous right hand"* (Isaiah 41:10).

So, although it's not always easy and often comes down to a choice:

- **CHOOSE** not to allow fear and anxiety to control your life.
- **CHOOSE** to guard your heart.
- **CHOOSE** to focus your mind on what truth is during uncertain times.

The Other Side of Me

"We might still feel afraid, but we can believe that God is with us. We may not be in control, but we can trust the One who is. We may not know the future, but we can know the God who does." (Crosswalk.com, BlogSpot for Debbie McDaniel of Fresh Day Ahead)

Through all I have experienced in my life, I still come back to this one thing: *"Yea, though I walk through the valley of the shadow of death, I will fear no evil. Your rod and Your staff, they comfort me. I can do all things through Christ that strengthens me. I have not been given the spirit of fear, but of power, and of love, and of a sound mind."* I know that God will keep me in perfect peace as I keep my mind stayed on Him. I don't have to walk in fear and anxiety. I don't have to run from the enemy, but I can run **TO** the One who created me. His name is Jesus Christ and in Him is where I can find rest. He's there when I need Him—day or night. He died on the cross for our sins, and everything that is connected to it [sin] was nailed to the cross. Therefore, I don't have to walk around fearful and paralyzed in every step I take.

We must let God fight our battles and, if need be, refer to what His Word says about us.

We are fearfully and wonderfully made.

We are the head and not the tail.

We are above, not beneath.

We were chosen from the very foundation of the Earth.

Therefore, my friend, we are **HIS**. When we gave our lives to Him, Paul tells us in Romans 8:17-18 that *"we became joint heirs to His throne. Therefore, if we suffer with Him, we may also be glorified together. For I consider that the sufferings of this present time are not worthy to be compared with the glory which shall be revealed in us."*

Paul then tells us that we have the victory in Jesus in Romans 8:37: *"Yet in all these things, we are more than conquerors through Him who loved us. For I am persuaded that neither death nor life, nor angels nor principalities, nor power nor things present nor things to come, nor height nor depth, nor any other created thing, shall be able to separate us from the love of God which is in Christ Jesus our Lord."* We conquer not by our own ability, but because God loves us.

We have the power to call out that mounted generational curse or lingering, nasty sin. We can send it back to the pits of Hell from whence it came. We don't have to succumb to what the enemy has thrown in front of us. Again, it's just another one of the fear tactics that he uses to try to knock us off-course by driving a wedge between God and us. He can only do what God **ALLOWS** him to do. If you don't believe me, read the book of Job! When we start to play into the devil's game or give him power or credit over something that God may have allowed him to do, we must stop and look at it in the spiritual realm—not the natural. You see, the Bible reminds us in Ephesians 6:12, *"For we wrestle not against flesh and blood, but against principalities, against powers, against the ruler of the darkness of this world, against spiritual wickedness in high places…"*

You don't have to stay in the situation you're in. You have a God who loves you with an unconditional love that **NO** man has. Why? Because God's love is everlasting. Man can love you today and hate you tomorrow. God's love never changes. He said that he would never put more on us than we can bear, so if you're going through a turbulent storm in your life, why not go to the Master who is All-Knowing and All-Powerful — the One who can fix *ALL* things? He's just waiting for you to come to Him. He already knows our flaws and struggles. He's not going to criticize us for our wrong behavior, but He will chastise us when we're wrong. This is how He shows us that He loves us: He will give us peace during our storms as He works it out. He will keep us in perfect peace if we just keep our mind stayed on Him.

*"And let us not be weary in well-doing;
for, in due season, we shall reap if we faint not."*
(Galatians 6:9)

Philippians 4:8 tells us that *"an idle mind is the devil's playground."* If he has your mind, he may very well have you. Sin begins in the mind. You get an idea or thought and begin to start playing the "What If? Game." Your "What if?" turns into curiosity. Your curiosity turns into playing with fire and, before you know it, you're consumed and wondering how you got there.

In reverse, you don't have to act out or do anything in any way to sin. It comes so easily and naturally to us that we don't even realize it is happening most of the time. In this state is where we allow our minds to store an enormous amount of sinful activity and thoughts because it's a safe place. We can choose to disclose certain information or none at all. We can walk around pretending that all is well. However, we must remember that we may have the ability to fool man, but there's no fooling God. He knows us because He's the one who created us.

To you (man/woman), I can smile in your face while my mind is in its full sinful realm, and you would be none the wiser because I've learned the "Art of Deception." I can greet you with a half-hearted *"Amen, brother/sister"* and a stand-offish hug, all while eying the quickest exit door because I don't want you or anyone else to get up close and personal about my lifestyle. I could easily pull out the *"only God can judge me"* card or the *"For all have sinned and fallen short of the glory of God"* scripture while feeling justified in saying those things. Still, in my heart of hearts, I know that I need to get right with God but would rather wrestle with the thought of feeling like God is a God of second chances instead of getting it right with Him the first go-around. It's like using His grace and mercy as a 'safety net' on the back burner for that 'last-minute life-altering event.'

An idle mind is an undisciplined and wandering mind. As Christians, we need to be disciplined in every area of our lives, for it is the thoughts that run through our mind that control our actions. The mind is a powerful thing and a wonderful tool, but it can also be a dangerous snare.

As I mentioned before, it is my hope that I can shed some light on my life's experiences to help someone else in the process know how they can come out of a storm in their life. No one can tell your story better than you. It is my prayer that if you have something in your life that you need to deal with, what better way is there than to ask God to give you a sense of direction as to how you should deal with it?

Chapter Eight

Tugging on the Skirt-Tail of My Sister

Friday night church services

Every Friday night was church service. If none of my other siblings were going, I knew I was for sure. It was something that my sister and I looked forward to. My sister, Bettye, would always take me with her, and I would play the drums during service. I found myself having a love for the church and always wanting to hear the Word of God. My pastor's preaching was rather intriguing. He was a sharp dresser, mild-mannered, and very fatherly. He and his sons were the musicians of the house and, when my brothers and I would show up, the pastor would quietly excuse himself from the organ because it meant that he could relax, enjoy the service, and listen to the Word being brought forth by other ministers.

Our church was very family-oriented and spirit-filled. The pastor believed in everyone living right. He didn't seem to care about how talented we were if we weren't living right. It seemed like Altar Call was in session every time for many of us because, on Sunday morning, the kids would sneak out of the church and run down the street to buy candy. We would use the "bathroom break" card to get us out the door, while one of us would be the lookout guy to summon the rest of us to the front door when it was safe to get past the female ushers.

Somehow, some way, we would manage to get halfway past the preaching and back to our seats without our parents flipping out. In the Early Church days, people reverenced the House of God more than we did…

I am most grateful to God that my mom — the Matriarch of our family — laid the foundation for us to know Christ. He allowed my sister Bettye to set the platform for our family by living an exemplified, holy lifestyle and running the race, only to give our family hope in knowing who Jesus Christ is. She has been a beacon of light to us all and has carried the torch for our family in hopes that one day, we would carry the torch for our families. I had finally found something that was worth me sticking to.

It's interesting because it wasn't something that was forced on me. Bringing souls to the House of God made a difference in my life. By the time I had graduated from high school, I was convinced that this would be my life. Even with facing opposition in her own life, my sister never gave up. She remained the glue that held us all together, all while raising a family of her own. I owe a debt of gratitude to her.

"The battle is not given to the swift nor the strong, but to he who endures to the end."
(Ecclesiastes 9:11)

"I beseech ye, brethren, by the mercies of God, that you present your bodies a living sacrifice…"
(Romans 12:1-2)

Chapter Nine

Dealing with Fear and Rejection

I've always had a fear of succeeding in life because of the many failed adventures. It felt like I had black darts coming at me from every direction. I could always just about sense when rejection and failure were coming my way. I would try so hard to grin and bear it, when deep down inside, I wanted to crawl under a rock.

Throughout my life, I've had people say to me, *"Keith, you probably won't be able to get into college because you must have a certain GPA"* or *"If I were you, I wouldn't put all my eggs in one basket. A good buddy of mine dropped out of college because he said he couldn't afford it. He said he made more money on the street than going to college and paying for a career that's not even guaranteed once you graduate."*

Now, imagine working alongside someone every day — someone you share all of your dreams and aspirations with **(BIG MISTAKE)** — in hopes of getting some encouragement to dream big. Then, for every positive dart you throw, they're shooting it down with **THREE** negatives. I believe that if you stick around a person long enough, they'll show you who they really are…especially when they start speaking to you in the third party **ABOUT** you. It's not enough for them to just come right out and tell you that they can't stand you and the ground you walk on; they'll even go to great lengths to get **OTHERS** not to want to have anything to do with you for fear that you'll excel beyond where they are. Usually, that's only because they're not happy with themselves or the way their life has turned out.

The crazy thing about it all is that while I was going out of my way to try to be a good friend to those people, I found out late in the game that the majority of them were not willing to reciprocate for me. So, it was good for them to be on the receiving end, while my needs went unmet. I had begun to dislike and lose trust in people who made me feel like our relationship was one-sided.

Don't get me wrong: I wasn't **LOOKING** for anything in return, but every now and then, it would've been nice to know that my so-called **"FRIENDS"** had my back in a dilemma. That why Psalm 118:3 says, *"It is better to trust in the Lord than to put trust in man."* Man is human and will let you down. God is a man that **HE** cannot lie.

"…being confident of this very thing, that He which hath begun a good work in you will perform it until the day of Jesus Christ."
(Philippians 1:6)

So, how do you bounce back from all of that when you've prayed to God for an answer and feel like you're all alone? The Bible tells us in Ephesians 6:13, *"Wherefore, take unto you the whole armor of God, that ye may be able to withstand in the evil day, and having done all, to stand."*

The Other Side of Me

Now, let's make it perfectly clear that I am not throwing my personal beliefs onto anyone. You're just the listener here; I am the venter. Getting that off my chest actually felt great!

For many years now, I have been longing to tell my story in hopes that it would not only free myself but also help those who may be struggling in the shoes in which I've walked due to this agonizing disease that has crippled me in more ways than one. I had been given multiple signs that I needed help ever since I was a child. I was clueless about how to deal with this "thing" because it was something I didn't understand.

What is this "thing," you ask?

You see, I spent over 30 years fighting a lustful spirit that had tightened its grip on every part of my life. Everywhere I turned, it was right there. It was there morning, noon, and night as a reminder that I would serve as a slave to it. It would send me on a spiraling road, causing me to test my faith and question whether or not I had a true relationship with God. I ran from the calling God had placed on my life and turned down the road of what seemed to be a point of no return.

That same spirit would silence and taunt me while in the presence of my family, friends, and fellow church members. I would often feel unclean and unworthy of being around the saints, yet I still called myself "saved." We all know that when you're sick, you go to the hospital because the doctor is the one who prescribes the medication for us to get better. And so, just like the woman with the 12-year issue of blood, she knew that if only she could touch the hem of Jesus' garment, she would be made whole (see Luke 8:43-48).

Another familiar biblical story (for some) would be of a blind beggar named Bartimaeus who was sitting on the side of the road as Jesus and His disciples were leaving Jericho. A large crowd followed them and, when the beggar heard Jesus from Nazareth was coming, he shouted, *"Jesus, son of David, have pity on me!"*

Imagine going to church and laying it all out on the line at the altar. You cry out to God and ask for deliverance, only to discover that you left the doctor's office (in this instance, the church) with the same sick symptoms that you walked in the door with. How depressing is that? The average person would probably try another hospital they thought could treat their symptoms correctly or provide them with a different report or better outcome than the last.

Well, much to my surprise, I learned that it wasn't the Healer who was to blame; I was the one nursing my wounds by placing a bandage over them instead of allowing God to work on me.

Note to self: *You **CANNOT** rebandage old wounds. They need time to heal.* ~**Keith Hughes** ~

So, now that we're all "in the know," why don't we just get it all out in the open and come clean so that someone's son or daughter can be liberated by the end of this book? (That's just a thought!)

You see, prior to my writing this book, I asked God to show me who I was in Him—not my wife, not my children, not my family members…just show me **ME**. Often, we hear people say, *"Be careful what you ask for…you just might get it!"* Well, that statement seemed to hold true in my life because what God revealed to me was hardly what I expected.

Let's admit it: We all have something in our past (or even our present) that we're not so proud of. In some instances, we wish that we could somehow instantly make it disappear.

POOF! BE GONE!

No one wants to be continuously reminded of how bad they screwed up and be made to feel like less of a person.

I was "that ugly guy" who was tormented by his past with uncontrollable cravings. I had addictions to porn websites, unprotected sex, one-night stands, masturbation, drinking, smoking weed, lying, fear of people's perception of me, fear of ministry, and the spirit of suicide. I even found myself becoming strongly addicted to women's feet. As strange and demonic as that may sound, it was my reality for years.

I often asked God, *"Why me? Why do I have to suffer from all of these clingy demonic forces?"* I had already failed at just about everything I put my hand to, so what exactly was my purpose in life? Who would want a washed-up has-been who couldn't hold down a job to save his life, had a music career that had gone belly-up, and contended with his flesh that was spiraling out of control? How in the world was I even surviving through this façade?

Well, I was wearing my mask of deception while literally dressing up and carrying a briefcase with barely anything in it—all in an attempt to be socially accepted by my peers. It was a ploy designed to keep them from seeing right through me. All the while, no one knew about **"The Other Side of Me."** I couldn't bear the thought of being called onto the carpet about my lifestyle. That would've been too humiliating, to put it mildly.

So, like any other reasonable person would want to know, I pondered over the following:

What was I going to do with the rest of my life?

How was I going to survive?

How would I tell my family that coming back to Toledo and starting all over again would probably be my best option?

What would be the church's perception of me?

I made up in my mind that the 'spirit of denial' was going to be my story—and I was sticking to it. For me, it was going to be a game of "don't ask, don't tell."

I was tired of being broke, busted, and disgusted. I was tired of watching others around me prosper while I struggled with wondering how I was going to eat the next day or pay a bill. I wanted the good life. I wanted a piece of the American pie with minimal effort to work hard at getting it. I felt like I had paid my dues to society by being an upstanding model citizen in the working world of business and school systems. I, in essence, felt a strong sense of entitlement. I knew I wasn't heading to the bank to take out a loan for a downpayment on a house anytime soon. I knew there wasn't going to be a supermodel wife greeting me at the door of our home with a 3-car garage out back and kids. In my mind, that was living! Anything contrary to that was called "wishful thinking wealth" where you spend a lot of wasted time wishing to get to that type of prestige one day. I wanted to feel like I mattered…like I was somebody.

For me, it was about being happy for once in the moment. God reminds us about material possessions in Luke 12:15:

> *"And He said to them, 'Take care, and be on your guard against all covetousness, for one's life does not consist in the abundance of his possessions."*

The key word in that parable is "covetousness." Covetousness can make you envious of your neighbor's possessions if you're not careful. There's nothing wrong with admiring what one has, but when you start to take on a jealous spirit and question God about what you have and don't have in comparison to your neighbor, it then becomes idolatry— which means you need to repent. Why? Because you have placed material things at greater importance than God and **HIS** desires. Those "things" have become idols to you.

The eyes of man see only the outside. The eyes of God see what's in your **HEART**. When you pass up helping others to maintain an unnecessary lifestyle, you are in sin.

"But seek first the kingdom of God and His righteousness, and all these things shall be added to you."
(Matthew 6:33)

"But those who desire to be rich fall into temptation, into a snare, into many senseless and harmful desires that plunge people into ruin and destruction. For the love of money is the root of all kinds of evils. It is through this craving that some have wandered away from the faith and pierced themselves with many pangs [a sudden feeling of mental or emotional distress or longing; remorse]*."*
(1 Timothy 6:9-10)

It goes without saying that God wants the best for us. It is not His desire to break our spirits and cause us pain. Often, we think that God doesn't love us when we're hit with a little discomfort. When we experience difficult times or feel gut-wrenching inner pains and turmoil, we usually try to assign blame. We either say, *"The devil caused this"* or *"God caused this."* (The greater likelihood is this: The devil **CAUSED** it, and God *ALLOWED* it.)

Consider the Old Testament story of Job. He was a man who was *"blameless and upright; he feared God and shunned evil"* (Job 1:1) — yet God gave Satan permission to *"strike everything [Job] has, but not Job himself"* (Job 1:11). God allowed Job to suffer incredible loss for reasons that were God's alone. Throughout Job's pains and losses, however, God never abandoned him for even a moment. God knew each step of the way how greatly Job was being afflicted. Our sovereign God was overseeing the refining of Job.

The good news for us is that anytime we find ourselves being broken, our sovereign God is overseeing the refining processes of our lives! He sees the beginning and the end. He has a good future designed for us and, ultimately, Heaven is waiting to receive us. We can be sure that our period of brokenness is not the end but rather a passage and process to a rich, new beginning.

Yes, God knows. God is powerful, and He loves us.

Remember always that God loves you. He only wants the best for you. If He didn't, then He wouldn't have ever sacrificed His Only Begotten Son for us and promised us eternal life with Him. And because He IS love, it is the nature and character of God.

In hindsight, God was trying to get me to see that the pain, hurt, and fear I had experienced all of those years was necessary. It was all for my good and for His glory. He needed someone whom He could count on — someone He could trust — to pass the torch or baton (the Word, if you will) to a world that would one day need a Lord and Savior. I am forever grateful that He chose me as His vessel to fulfill His purpose.

The question *"Where would I be if it had not been for the Lord who was on my side?"* remains self-evident to me. I would probably be somewhere locked inside of a mental institution or behind bars for some heinous crime. I could have very easily been assigned to that car accident or drowned, as I've come close to those incidents many times before. The doctors could have told me that I was diagnosed with heart failure—the condition that claimed my father's life. I could've very well cut off the very breath in my body by taking my life as I contemplated jumping out of a bay window. So, you see, all of those things would have been the "easy way out." That means I would have died without fulfilling the purpose that God has for my life.

However, because of His grace and mercy that has sustained me thus far, I can say that I stand here today victorious, healed, delivered, and set free from sin because of the blood that was shed for me on the cross. It was at that very moment when I received the revelation of who God was in my life. God was trying to get something **TO** me—not *DESTROY* me. He allowed me to see so clearly that He wasn't trying to destroy me, just as He wasn't trying to destroy Job. I really needed Him, whether I cared to admit it or not. God realized that the **ONLY** way I would get what He had for me and have an appreciation for and hold onto it was that it was necessary for me to go through the storm that way. What am I talking about? I'm talking about His anointing. That's right: **His anointing.** God's anointing is not something we can purchase. It's priceless! And when you have it, you better guard it with your life.

Let's explore the meaning of "anointing" before moving along…

First, we must recognize that God anoints His people for a purpose! He anointed Jesus, and He anoints His children. Another way we can look at anointing is that we are called the "ones chosen." In other words, there is a calling on your life to spread the Good News (the Gospel of Jesus Christ) by sharing it with the lost, just as Jesus was anointed by God with the Holy Spirit to do the same (see Luke 4:18-19; Acts 10:38).

After Christ left the Earth, He gave us the gift of the Holy Spirit (see John 14:16). Now, all Christians are anointed and chosen for a specific purpose in furthering God's Kingdom (see 1 John 2:20).

> *"Now He who establishes us with you in Christ and has anointed us is God, who also sealed us and gave us the Spirit in our heart as a guarantee."*
> **(2 Corinthians 1:21-22)**

The anointing is symbolic of blessing, protection, and empowerment. It is the power to serve God.

What is God's anointing and how do you get it?

The anointing is the overflow of Christ in your life! It comes to us as we spend time in God's Word, seek Him with our whole heart, and worship Him. Jesus said, *"If ye abide in Me, and My words abide in you, ye shall ask what ye will, and it shall be done unto you"* (John 15:7). We increase the anointing by spending time in His presence.

Seven things the anointing will bring to you when you operate in it:

1. Healing. Restores your health (Luke 10:33-34).
2. Revelation. The anointing changes lives (Exodus 25:6).
3. Provision. Meets every need in your life (1 Kings 17:14).
4. Debt-free living. Causes the supernatural to happen for you to break free and clean financially (2 Kings 4:1-7).
5. Deliverance. To become delivered from your enemies (Psalm 23:1-5).
6. Faith. To be activated and released by the shield of faith because of the anointing (Psalm 133:3).
7. Blessings. He commands the blessings on you through His Word (2 Corinthians 1:20).

God cannot go back on His promise to us. He would be going against Himself if He did. That's impossible! **GOD CANNOT LIE!** It is His covenant to us. With this anointing, it gives us the power to change lives and influence nations. It is our opportunity to save lost and hurting souls by introducing them to Jesus Christ. In doing this, we can claim His promises.

What are God's promises?

The promises of God are "yes and amen" (see 2 Corinthians 1:20).

- ❖ Eternal Life
- ❖ Forgiveness
- ❖ Holy Spirit
- ❖ Money/Finances

- ❖ Our Needs
- ❖ Bible Promises for Healing
- ❖ Wisdom/Guidance
- ❖ Children, Family, and Marriage
- ❖ Peace
- ❖ Overcoming Temptation
- ❖ Protection
- ❖ Fear
- ❖ Resurrection
- ❖ End of Suffering

You see, I wouldn't wish some of my life's challenges on my worst enemies, but to God, I am a living witness that He can take that which was dead and bring it back to life. He is the Way, the Truth, and the Life; no man cometh unto the Father but by Christ (see John 14:6).

"But if ye should suffer for what is righteousness' sake, blessed are ye; but be not afraid of their fear, neither be troubled."
(1 Peter 3:14)

That passage of scripture means that we should count it as a privilege to suffer for a lifestyle that pleases God and, in return, He will reward you (see James 1:2).

God gives us specific instructions on how to cope when faced with tactics of the enemy to remain victorious: Put on the whole armor of God!

Keith Hughes

"Put on the whole armor of God, that ye may be able to stand against the wiles of the devil.

For we wrestle not against flesh and blood, but against principalities, against powers, against the rulers of the darkness of this world, against spiritual wickedness in high places.

Wherefore, take unto you the whole armor of God, that ye may be able to withstand in the evil day, and having done all, to stand.

Stand, therefore, having your loins girt about you with truth, and having on the breastplate of righteousness;

And your feet shod with the preparation of the gospel of peace;

Above all, taking the shield of faith, wherewith ye shall be able to quench all the fiery darts of the wicked.

And take the helmet of salvation, and the sword of the Spirit, which is the Word of God:

Praying always with all prayer and supplication in the Spirit, and watching thereunto with all perseverance and supplication for all saints."
(Ephesians 6:11-18)

So, who is this great **GOD** that we serve?

- He is the King ruler of everything.
- He is the King of kings.
- He is the Lord of lords.
- He is the Great I Am.
- He is the Great El Shaddai.
- He is the Great Elohim.
- He is Jehovah Jireh.
- He is Jehovah Rapha.
- He is Jehovah Sit Canoe.
- He is the One who's All-Powerful; All-Knowing.
- He is the Beginning and the End.
- He is the Alpha and Omega.
- He is the One who created the Heavens and the Earth.
- He is the One who blew the breath of life into Adam and Eve; He created man.
- It is in **HIM** that I have my being.

"So, we continue to preach Christ to each person, using all wisdom to warn and to each everyone, to bring each one into God's presence as a mature person in Christ."
(Colossians 1:28)

When we start to look at things from God's perspective, we begin to understand why He does what He does. We begin to realize that it is a part of our spiritual growth. Perspective is understanding something because you see things from a larger frame of reference. It is the ability to perceive how things are interrelated and then judge their comparative importance.

In a spiritual sense, it means seeing life from God's point of view. In the Bible, the words "understanding," "wisdom," and "discernment" all related to perspective. The opposite of perspective is "hardness of heart," "blinded," and "dullness."

Psalm 103:7 says, *"He [God] made known His ways to Moses, His deeds to the people of Israel."* The people of Israel were able to see what God did, but Moses obtained an understanding of **WHY** God did it. That is the difference between knowledge and perspective. **Knowledge** is learning what God has said and done. **Perspective** understands why God said or did it.

Perspective answers the "Why?" question of life. The Bible says that unbelievers have no spiritual perspective (see 1 Corinthians 2:14). Likewise, a lack of perspective is a mark of spiritual immaturity (see 1 Corinthians 3:1-2, 13:11, 14:20).

In contrast, having perspective is evidence of spiritual maturity. Hebrews 5:14 says, *"But solid food is for the mature, who, because of practice, have their senses trained to discern good and evil."* There are many benefits of learning to see everything from God's perspective.

- Perspective causes us to love God more. The better we understand the nature and ways of God, the more we love Him. Paul prayed, *"May you be able to feel and understand, as all God's children should, how long, how wide, how deep, and how high His love really is"* (Ephesians 3:18).
- Perspective helps us resist temptation. When we look at a situation from God's viewpoint, we realize the long-term consequences of sin are greater than any short-term

pleasure that sin might provide. Without perspective, we follow our natural inclinations. *"There is a way that appears to be right, but in the end, it leads to death"* (Proverbs 14:12).

- Perspective helps us handle trials. When we have God's perspective on life, we realize that *"in all things, God works for the good of those who love Him"* (Romans 8:28) and that the *"testing of your faith develops perseverance"* (James 1:3). Perspective was one of the reasons Jesus could endure the cross (see Hebrews 12:2). He looked past the pain and saw the joy that was set before Him.
- Perspective protects us from error. If ever there was a time that Christians need to be rooted and grounded in the truth, it is today. Pluralism has created a very confused culture. The problem is not that our culture believes nothing; instead the issue is that it believes everything. Perspective is the antidote.

When believers—new and mature—are given both knowledge and perspective, the result is rock solid: *"Then we will no longer be like children, forever changing our minds about what we believe because someone has told us something different or has cleverly lied to us and made the lie sound like the truth"* (Ephesians 4:14).

Whose report will you believe for your healing?

"Success isn't measured by money or power or social rank. Success is measured by your discipline and inner peace."
~ Mike Ditka ~

Throughout all that I had endured, I had no inner peace. So, how was I going to find peace—the Lord Jesus Christ—within when all hell had broken loose in my life?

I am reminded of the parable of the return of the Prodigal Son. In the story, a father had two sons. The younger son asked for his inheritance and, after wasting his fortune (the word 'prodigal' means "wastefully extravagant"), he became destitute. He returned home with the intention of begging his father to be made one of his hired servants, expecting that his relationship with his father was likely severed. Oh, but God! The father welcomed him back and celebrated his return! The older son refused to participate. The father reminded the older son that one day, he would inherit everything, but they should still celebrate the return of the younger son because he was lost but was now found.

Chapter Ten

Introducing My Secret to My Parents

I remember it just like it was yesterday... Now, in my defense, before my dad died, I tried taking my issue to both him and my mom to see if they could give me some clear insight as to what was going on with me. My parents were sitting downstairs in the living room talking about the renovations to one of their properties. I politely excused myself and asked for their undivided attention, not knowing what the consequences would be. I just figured, *"Well, it's now or never!"*

As I began to share my story, both sat quietly without any interruptions. Their faces held blank stares that could have possibly killed a cat. As I was wrapping things up, my mom quickly interrupted me and asked, *"How long has this been going on?"* I responded, *"Since I was six years old – and I hate it! I wish it would just go away."* Dad looked at me with a smile of relief. He was glad I didn't drop a bomb on him that I was "coming out of the closet." He didn't care for gays at all. He thought it was the most disgusting thing on the face of the Earth...or so it seemed.

Mom, on the other hand, replied to me by saying, *"Well, Keith; if this is the big secret that you've been dealing with all this time, then you're fine. There are so many people who deal with the same thing that you deal with but refuse to tell anybody. As quiet as it's kept, I would rather you masturbate than put your mouth down there on a woman."*

Immediately, my eyes became as big as the confession I just made! I needed to be sure I heard her correctly, so I asked her, *"What do you mean by that?"*

My dad sat up on the couch with this cheesy, sheepish, dark grin on his face as if he had been **WAITING** to give me a class on oral sex. I tried hard not to imagine what may have been going through his mind, so I quickly refocused my attention on my mom. Somehow, I knew I was safe with my personal issue after looking at him.

Mom continued. *"Boy, I don't see how any man could ever put his mouth down there on a woman. That is the nastiest, most disgusting thing that any man or woman could ever do!"*

For a moment, I thought there was going to be a point to all of this as she continued by saying, *"Men pee, sweat, scratch themselves, and stick their privates in any and everything that walks with two legs. For the life of me, I don't see how anybody could stick their mouth down there and expect **ME** to kiss you afterward. Noooo!"*

Well, after **THAT** nasty description of oral sex coming from my mom, masturbation seemed to no longer be a big deal! I just wanted her to stop talking about it because dad looked like he had a whole different take on the subject. With that grin that stayed plastered across his face, I certainly did **NOT** want to hear his take on it. I did **NOT** want the images from his version stuck in my head.

I politely thanked them both for the "oral sex education class" and looked for the nearest exit. Dad's two cents followed me out the door: *"Son, you gon' be alright. Don't worry about it. A lot of people go through that when they're growing up. It ain't gon' kill ya!"* As shocked as I was with how the conversation went, I had expected more coming from them. They weren't upset nor bothered that their son had an ongoing, mind-controlling sex addiction.

I think my parents were leaving it up to me to figure out how to stop my "behavior" because they didn't have an answer or "magical wand" to wave it away. So, I guess that was their way of saying, *"We've all done something in life that we're not proud of, but it's not what you've done…it's how you come out of it that makes the difference."* Unfortunately, I was left with an issue that was like a monkey clinging to my back and wouldn't let go of me. I started to believe my parents just weren't nurturers because my comfort and safety were ultimately found in spending time with my sisters, Bettye and Pat.

My parents spent more time working and hammering on their properties than they did getting to know their kids. I think it's safe to say I know absolutely nothing about my father's side of the family and little about my mom's side because we didn't visit them "like that." Most of them lived down south, so when we did visit them, it was hard for us kids to address everyone by their correct name. To no fault of my own, I remember having a slight crush on my cousin—until I found out that we were cousins. That was demonstrative of how little we knew our family...

In the Book of James (1:8, 4:8), the Apostle James uses the term "double-minded." Double-minded is a problem that can be damaging to Christians and can manifest itself in several areas of their lives. The Greek word for "double-minded" is *dipsuchos* from *'dis,'* meaning "twice," and *'psuche,'* meaning "mind." James uses it to describe someone who is divided in his interests or loyalties, wavering, uncertain, two-faced, and half-hearted. The word "fear" can be thought of by the acronym:

F – False

E – Evidence

A – Appearing

R – Real

The War Within: Flesh vs. Spirit

Fear had paralyzed me in every area of my life imaginable when it came to relationships, jobs, ministry, and interacting with people in general. Being shy was my cover-up—my way of shutting down when I felt the spirit of fear weighing on me. I knew deep down inside that I had greatness in me, but the spirit of fear was winning over my ability to have love, power, and a sound mind. My thoughts and actions were all over the place. You could say that yes, I was double-minded in **ALL** my ways.

The Other Side of Me

I was operating in ministry on Sunday morning and by 5:00 p.m. that same day, I was fornicating, masturbating, drinking, trying my hand at smoking marijuana, and chasing women. All the while, I still proclaimed the Gospel of Jesus Christ and asked God to cover me in the act of sinning. My mind and body had **NO** shame. It wanted what it wanted, when it wanted it, where it wanted it, and how it wanted it. The outcome or circumstances were going to be as they were…dangling on the "string of life or facing death."

My life had plummeted into total darkness with no chance of seeing my way out. By the time Saturday night came, I had found myself pleading with and asking God to forgive me of my sins. I needed another chance at getting it right before my next "Sunday morning circus act!"

This is as real as it gets, folks. I told you at the beginning of this book that it would be the raw, naked truth—known as the "Tell-All" to both free myself as well as help someone else.

At altar call, it was me who always stood in constant need of prayer, although I wasn't going to admit it. I would sing, *"No weapon formed against me shall prosper; it won't work,"* with the translation running through my mind that said, ***"But I saw every dart imaginable being thrown at me."***

More words from the song are: *"God will do what He said He would do. He will stand by His Word; He will come through."*

My translation: ***"Well, when is He coming? These bills are due! I need food on the table and gas in my car! These bills*** *aren't going to pay themselves, and my good looks aren't going to fill up my freezer!"*

See? I was nothing short of a mental case waiting to happen. All I needed at the time was a white straight jacket and a padded room. Clearly, I was lacking in patience and had lost the victory in two verses of that song. The song challenged me to activate my faith, as I lacked profoundly in that area while operating in sin daily. To make a long story short, I was the "Spiritually Walking Dead." I had no real relationship with God. I was powerless and open for any vulnerable attack imaginable.

It was easy for me not to trust God because everyone around me had proven to me that they couldn't be trusted. That left me feeling alone and like I had to get out there and get my needs and desires met on my own. Prayer had become a serious joke because it seemed like I had adopted a pattern: I would pray and ask God to move on my behalf, and it never failed that He would let me down once again.

I hated church songs, too. They were all speaking the same language of how good God was, yet I wasn't seeing Him manifest Himself in my life at all. I didn't see any fruit. I simply didn't believe much in the power of God, prayer, or anything else for that matter. So, I would turn the radio off or tune in to an R&B station.

My thoughts were, *"God doesn't love me the way that He loves others. He has His certain picks and apparently, I am not good enough to make the 'Holier Than Thou' cut. Why should I go around toting the Bible and professing to know Him when, for one, I don't understand the Bible; for two, I don't get Him; and three, I am certainly not going to serve something or someone that I can't see!"*

At the time, I wished I had never been introduced to Jesus Christ because He just seemed like He was too much drama to deal with.

Again, let me make it perfectly clear that those were my thoughts as I was growing up and coming into truly knowing who He was in my life.

Chapter Eleven

Fighting Fear

For a long time, I had a strong sense of fear of people, the church, and ministry. Anyone who knows me knows that I am not very confrontational. I would rather talk and try to reason with you than going to blows. I'm just cut from that kind of cloth. However, for me, it was most intimidating to see others operating in their God-given gifts when I was still trying to figure out how to perfect just **ONE** of mine. The difference was that it seemed like they were experts on how to speak and lead the congregation into God's presence by knowing what to say, how to say it, and when to say it. I, on the other hand, felt ill-prepared (in every sense of the word) every time I stepped foot through the church's doors and around people of God in general.

I didn't know how to pray. I didn't know what to pray for. I didn't know anything about strongholds or a strongman. I couldn't bear the thought of the saints thinking that I was dumb for not having a close relationship with God, as maybe some of them had. Of course, there were those saints who seemed like they knew every praise and worship song ever written and every scripture of all 66 Books of the Bible. How could I possibly compete with that? I couldn't!

However, I did know what "binding" meant because it was so well-rehearsed in all the prayers that went forth. Therefore, if I could just make it through the service without getting attention, I knew I'd be home free! Fear of not being able to comprehend who God is and His Word left me feeling spiritually crippled, for lack of a better word. If you've never been there, it is the most embarrassing and humiliating form of torture one could ever experience.

Call it "mind over matter" if you will, but my stomach was always in knots for fear that my pastor would call on me to pray during the beginning of service or participate in the service in some form or fashion. It wasn't that I didn't want to be active; I just didn't understand who God was because the truth of the matter is…I really didn't know Him. I only knew *OF* Him. I didn't want to sing songs that had very little meaning to me. I wanted to know what I was singing about. How was I going to exhort and give others encouraging words to live by when I couldn't even provide scriptural facts to back up what I was even singing about?

Fear was winning hands down over my faith on every level, and I allowed it because I was too afraid that I would get a real revelation of who God really was. This meant that I would probably get exposed for who I really was and get called onto the carpet about my walk with Him. I was honestly fearful of real deliverance…and the naysayers. I was left feeling like an imposter in the church. I didn't want to spend an hour at the altar foaming at the mouth and chanting, *"Jesus, Jesus, Jesus, Jesus! Hallelujah, Hallelujah, Hallelujah, Hallelujah!"* while hearing mothers of the church yelling in my ear from every direction. Getting delivered from sin, having the evidence of speaking in tongues, and going down in Jesus' name was just too fearful for me.

My sinful appetite was quickly kicking in by the time service was ending. My mind was telling me that I needed to relieve myself like a crack addict needed drugs for that ultimate high. I was so discombobulated and miserable because I was tired of getting dressed to the 'T,' going to church as usual, and getting nothing out of it. I was wasting my own time but didn't know how to make myself stay away from the church doors. There was something there for me and somehow, some way, I had to get it. To no one's fault of their own, I sat in envy, desiring the fire connection that others had for God but was too afraid to get for myself.

The "Fear of Man" is something to be reckoned with. It can do a number on you if you give it too much attention. Many of us never reach our full potential because we allow man to be dictators and rulers over our lives instead of God. It never truly hit me that my naysayers were no better than me when it came to my growth in God. What I mean by that is this: Sometimes, the ones who are throwing stones are the ones who wish they had the power that you possess. Why? Because of the anointing and calling that's on your life. It can be intimidating, especially when that other person feels there is a strong potential that you will take the "spotlight" or position they think they're qualified to have, whether they've been called to operate in that area of ministry or not. It's a 'territorial mindset' that we get when we feel the dangers of another moving in on our turf.

The Other Side of Me

Here's the thing: They see the anointing on your life—but you don't. The reason why **YOU** don't see it is because, in your heart, you've already gotten in your head that they've mastered the 'Art of Ministry.' Therefore, you don't think you belong in that arena. They very well may even suck at it, but here is the difference between you and them: You both have two separate levels of fear.

- ❖ The naysayer fears that you'll come in and "do ministry" better than them. You will win souls.
- ❖ You fear that you don't want to be a major disappointment to God, the pastor, or the congregation. This shows that you at least have the heart to do right.
- ❖ Some are in it to serve the pastor, not God. They feel if they can pull on the coattail of the pastor, it will skyrocket them forward into a ministry of their own or bring special clout or recognition to their name.
- ❖ The adversary comes to kill, steal, and destroy. So, if you're bombarded with the distractions of naysayers, you're setting up camp for the adversary to play with your mind and tell you that you are a failure, nothing ever goes right for you, others around you are blessed while you continue to struggle, and you don't have the right to be the Pastor's Assistant. Your place is sitting in the pews and fanning yourself while God continues to use you in your "idle mindset"—and you're okay with that, as long as you don't get exposed.

So, you see how this scenario plays out when we give the adversary way too much thought when we should be seeking God to get a clear divine revelation? Ultimately, only what you and I do for Christ will last. This tells us that what our naysayers say, think, and feel about us doesn't amount to a hill of beans. They're not the ones you're going to have to answer to. They don't have a Heaven or Hell to put you in. So, don't trip! Get on board with **GOD** and find your place in Him. Work the ministry to your fullest potential. Remember: God takes care of His own!

> *"'Do not be afraid of them,*
> *for I am with you to deliver you,' declares the Lord."*
> **(Jeremiah 1:8)**

Your walk with God should not be predicated on the fact that you're trying to be in right standing with Him; it should be that you have the heart to want to live for Him and give 100% of yourself to the best of your human ability.

I'm all on board for sitting down and being taught what true ministry is all about. I believe I've been that way since I was a kid. I have never been one who volunteered as the **"Ooo, me! Me! Me!"** position-seeker. It's never been that serious to me. I believe that we become better leaders when we possess the core values of character, integrity, dignity, honesty, and a well-structured home base followed by a good old biblical foundation. If these values are implemented in our daily walk, then there is a high possibility that we have 'Spiritual Ammunition' to fight with when the storms of life show their ugly faces.

I must pause here to state this: Everyone doesn't come from a home that had a loving background. Many of us did not allow our circumstances to dictate how life was going to turn out. Somewhere in the middle of our impoverished state, we made the conscious decision that this world would not become our fate. We knew that someday, somehow there had to be something greater out there in store for us; we just had to go get it.

With life's ups and downs, we learn how to adapt to whatever is thrown at us quickly. We're able to go back and use some of the core values we've been taught as a way of implementing survival skills. Our skills come from those influential leaders who are and have been the 'Inspirational Delegates' who have paved the way for us since birth, to include:

- ✓ Parents
- ✓ Teachers
- ✓ Coaches
- ✓ Pastors
- ✓ Inspirational/Activist leaders such as Dr. Martin Luther King, Jr., Malcolm X, Rosa Parks, Harriet Tubman, and Marcus Garvey, Jr. — just to name a few of my own sources of inspiration.

So, you see, we've all aspired to be like someone or something at one point in our lives. The seed was planted, and it was up to us to water it.

"We are the change that we want to see."
~ Keith Hughes ~

When we learn how to operate well in those core values, we learn how to become trustworthy leaders who can pull up another when we see that person can improve in areas where there is some weakness. It doesn't label them as a bad person or any less smart; it just means this is our opportunity to share our profound knowledge that makes us all winners in the end.

Believe it or not, some level of fear is good for you. It keeps you well-grounded all the way around. Fear has its rightful place in many ways when applied correctly. For example, the very thought of fear may immediately trudge up images of horror films, losing a job, or feeling the loss of a lifelong, blissful marriage. I found out that after all the years I lived in fear, the person I feared the most was **ME**.

I feared the feeling of defeat before it happened. I feared being asked to speak, read, or give a presentation in front of the class or during Bible study. I feared singing a solo, all while thinking of ten different reasons why I could not do it (it was the most terrifying, gut-wrenching act that anyone could ask of me). In the end, I hated myself for believing I ***COULDN'T*** do it. I would think to myself, *"The other person who went along with the request obviously had more preparation time than I did. They were the better pick."* My lack of preparation spoke volumes.

2 Timothy 2:15 tell us to *"Study to shew thyself approved unto God, a workman that needed not to be ashamed, rightly dividing the Word of Truth."*

2 Timothy 4:2 tells us to *"Preach the Word; be instant in season, out of season; reprove, rebuke, exhort with all longsuffering and doctrine."*

In other words, we should 'be ready' — whether we feel like it or not.

"If we do only what we feel inclined to do, some of us would never do anything. There are some people who are spiritually feeble and weak, and they refuse to do anything unless they are supernaturally inspired. The proof that our relationship with God is that we do our best, whether we feel inspired or not."
~ **Wisdom from Oswald Chambers** ~

Oswald's word of wisdom hit me like a sack of nickels. Never did it make more sense than just reading it as if it were my first time. In all of this, each of our leaders has been saying for years, *"Stay ready, so you don't have to get ready!"* You may never know when your time is coming when you will be called upon for a contribution to ministry. It is not the preacher's job to get you ready; it's yours. He/She merely aids you in the areas of ministry. It is your job to prepare, just as you would for a test, a job interview, or a promotion.

Now, let's flip the script.

What does faith say about fear? Faith and fear cannot exist together. Faith is described in Hebrews 11:1 as being *"certain of what we do not see."* Faith is an absolute belief that God is continually working behind the scenes in every area of our lives, even when there is no tangible evidence to support that fact.

On the other hand, fear—simply stated—is unbelief or weak belief. As unbelief gains the upper hand in our thoughts, fear takes hold of our emotions.

Our deliverance from fear and worry is based on faith, which is the very opposite of unbelief. We need to understand that faith is not something we can produce ourselves. Faith is a gift (see Ephesians 2:8-9), which is described as a fruit (or characteristic) produced in our lives by the Holy Spirit (see Galatians 5:22-23).

One of the ways we can develop faith in conquering our fears can be found in Romans 10:17.

"Faith comes by hearing, and hearing by the Word of God."

The study of God's Word is of primary importance in developing a strong faith. God wants us to know Him and completely rely on His direction in our lives. It's through the hearing and reading of the Scriptures and meditating on them that we begin to experience a strong, confident faith that excludes worry and fear.

We can be whoever God wants us to be if we're willing to put in the work and give Him our all. He does not expect us to be perfect. He knows we won't get it 100% correct every single time. Just the heart of wanting to do what's right can and will capture the very essence of God. So, thirst after Him.

The Other Side of Me

I cannot stress how much better I feel these days, knowing that Christ carried my burdens on His shoulders as He stumbled to Calvary on my behalf. All excuses were nailed to the cross for my sake. There should be no reason why I could not give my life to Him.

It goes without saying that we are, indeed, a blessed people who have so much to be grateful for, yet we often struggle with seeing that in both the spiritual and natural sense. It is sometimes beyond the realms of possibility to expect people to trust God when their "right now answer" is unknown. It's the waiting process that gets us.

Through it all, I was able to get back on track with God and develop a true relationship with Him—one I had longed to have. Every day isn't glitter and gold, but it **IS** much sweeter than the day before. What a friend we have in Jesus! I was able to heal from my past hurt and realize that people are who they are. We cannot expect everyone to change simply because we think they should. No one is perfect. Only one holds the key to my salvation...***GOD!***

There's no good reason to go through life holding onto grudges about situations I cannot change. I think it's best just to let it run its course and, eventually, it will die out. No one is beyond change, but again, it must be in your heart to want it if you seek a better life. I cannot stress enough that **YOU** control your destiny. **YOU** have the key to close the door to Satan's devices. The Apostle Paul tells us, *"Don't be ignorant of Satan's devices."* We are at war! Satan hates us and wants to destroy us.

We must be aware of our enemy's weapons and tactics because our spiritual life depends on it (see 2 Corinthians 2:11).

One of Satan's most potent weapons against man is pride. Pride is always a danger, especially when things are going well, such as in times of peace and prosperity (see Deuteronomy 8:11). Perhaps the best example would be Lucifer himself—the one who became Satan. From the time of his creation, he had always lived under God's perfect rule. His heart then became lifted with pride, and he rebelled (see Isaiah 14:12-15; Ezekiel 28:14-17; 1 Timothy 3:6). He uses that same stronghold on us now.

If we look at the word "stronghold," we find that it is:

- A place that has been fortified to protect it against attack.
- Synonyms for stronghold include fortress, fort, castle, citadel, garrison, and **"the enemy's stronghold."**

Chapter Twelve

Walking Away from My Spiritual Covering

I was faced with a choice: Walk away or stay and walk out the uncomfortable journey with the church. Let me make it clear that it was no fault of the church or the pastor. The teaching and preaching I received were remarkable and life-changing. However, I didn't want to own up to the fact that I needed help in my spiritual walk. In my heart of hearts, I didn't want the church or my family's support. I wanted to remain in my dead relationship, but I also knew it would be difficult for me to explain why. I made a perilous move. I walked away from the ministry, my family, and all that I had accomplished because I wanted to be in a relationship that turned out to be "toxic."

Contrary to what we might think, God doesn't force Himself on us, which is why He gives us free will. When all is said and done, we will, without a shadow of a doubt, **ALL** bow down and worship Him. It really doesn't matter what our personal religious beliefs are. We can rest assured that on **THAT** day, He will be reverenced.

Well, I finally did it. I packed up my things without telling anyone and moved to Jeffersonville, Indiana to be with her. No one knew where I went until I called home and told them. As I'm sure you can imagine, that conversation did not go so well. I was told I was making the biggest mistake of my life by leaving from under my spiritual covering without telling my pastor — or seeking God's guidance.

As the months went on, I did not reach out to the pastor or church, but I did visit when I had an opportunity to do so. It was awkward, to say the least, because of the guilt I carried within. I knew I was wrong but didn't have the guts to ask for the pastor's forgiveness. Although he greeted me with love and compassion, the one thing I noticed was that he never questioned why I left. He would greet me with a smile, hug, and hearty *"God bless you!"* — followed with *"Come back and see us!"* Honestly, I expected more from him. I'm pretty sure my face seemed like it shattered into a million pieces as I pondered, *"Why won't he ask me about my whereabouts? Was he angry with me? Did he completely wash his hands of me? Was it the "one monkey doesn't stop the show" thought?"* Whatever it was (or wasn't), the bottom line was that I felt empty and disappointed in my actions. I was ready to run away again.

One of the things I love about my pastor is that he has adopted the saying, *"I'm not begging and pleading with anyone who doesn't want to be saved. There are way too many people who need Christ, and we're not babysitting people who don't want to get right."* **I LOVE IT!** What an awesome man of God! He is a tell-it-like-it-is pastor who doesn't cut corners for **ANYONE**. It's either Heaven or Hell. **YOU** choose. It's **YOUR** life!

The Other Side of Me

To expound more on the biblical parable of the Prodigal Son as recorded in Luke 15:11-32: There was a man who had two sons. The younger one said to his father, *"Father, give me my share of the estate."* So, the father divided his property between his two sons. Long after that, the younger son put together all he had, departed, and lost it all due to a wild lifestyle. After spending everything he had, a severe famine hit the entire country. He then went to work to feed pigs and longed to eat the keratin (the pods of the Carob trees were used as feed to fatten the pigs).

Once he realized that all he had was gone, he came to his senses and thinks, *"Maybe home is where I ought to be."* He decided to return and ask for his father's forgiveness. As he made his way back home, his father saw him from afar and welcomed him back with open arms and a feast of celebration. The story goes on to say that although the son didn't believe he was worthy of such a celebration or even to be called "his father's son," he begged for a position as a hired servant.

That parable is one of the three that proves God searches for the lost, whether that be a sheep, coin, or person.

How does the parable relate to my life? Well, God allowed me (a sinner) to go my separate way because He understands that we all possess a foolish ambition to be independent, which is at the root of the sinner persisting in sin. A sinful state is a departure and distancing from God (see Romans 1:21). A sinful state is also one of constant discontent.

I had taken for granted that God knew my heart while still wanting to live my life how I saw fit—only to see that things didn't work out so great on my behalf after all. My rock-bottom came after moving to Columbus, Ohio, losing three jobs, and dealing with my mom's failing health scare. I then moved back to Toledo and had to come face-to-face with my pastor and ask for his forgiveness. Again, he greeted me with a hearty handshake and hug. He was excited to know I had rededicated my life to Jesus Christ and, for the very first time, I introduced him and the congregation to my new wife. I announced that we were there to stay for the long haul and serve where God would have us.

Never once did the pastor throw the book at me or ridicule me for the mistakes I had made. He simply welcomed me, assured me that things were going to be okay and that it was time to get back to where God had called me to be. To this day, I am grateful to be a servant under this great man of God who cares deeply for his people, only desiring that we carry out our task in serving God wholeheartedly and bring others into the sheepfold of Christ.

Another popular Bible story is of Jesus and the Samaritan woman at the well (John 4:1-42). The story takes place at Jacob's Well, just outside the town of Sychar, while Jesus was waiting for His disciples to go in town to purchase food. A woman from Samaria came to draw water from the well. Jesus said to her, *"Give Me a drink."* Then, the woman said to Him, *"How is it that You, being a Jew, ask a drink from me, a Samaritan woman? For Jews have no dealings with Samaritans."* Jesus answered and said to her, *"If you knew the gift of God and who it is who says to you, 'Give Me a drink,' you would have asked Him, and He would have given you living water."*

Furthermore, Jesus lets the woman know that her current husband is not her own; neither were the others that she claimed. Once the Samaritan woman realized who she was talking to, she immediately runs and tells everyone, *"Come see a man who told me all the things I had ever done! Is he not the Christ?"*

In summation, Jesus knows all about us. There is nothing new to Him under the sun. He knows us inside and out. He knows the very number of hairs on our heads because He is just that detailed.

So, how much more will we allow Him to be involved in our lives?

Chapter Thirteen

The Abusive Relationship

In May 2000, I moved to Jeffersonville, Indiana. I entered a relationship with a single mother of two teenage children. That relationship lasted only three years because I discovered she had cheated on me while I was working at night.

Although I had strong feelings for her, the hurt, lies, and distrust were too much for me to deal with. To me, the relationship wasn't strong enough for me to stay, so we decided to cut ties. Shortly after the break-up, I came face-to-face with a brush of death that would forever change my life.

As time went on, I met a woman while doing ministry — only to find myself locked into an 8-year abusive relationship that resulted in me being repeatedly insulted. I was told that I was a "cry baby" and a "punk." I watched this woman go shopping, come home, shower, and get dressed to go out and spend the night with another man—leaving me home to watch her kids. That's right. I was her babysitter while she went out to the nightclubs and had affairs with other men.

I would call her when I realized the nightclub was closed. Where was she? Why didn't she contact me to let me know she was okay? My asking would send her into a frenzy. She would call me every cuss word imaginable and tell me not to worry about who she hung out with. When she finally returned home, she would fall completely silent, shower, get in bed, and in a matter of minutes, fall asleep. That would signal the end of the conversation.

By the next afternoon, she had already pre-determined that her infidelity was apparently my fault. She would tell me that I was the reason why she acted out. *"If only you would chill out and let me be who I am, then just maybe we could work out."* Wow! I could not believe that woman asked me to conform to her sinful lifestyle! That's not to say I was any better than she was, but I thought that was the most coldhearted, insulting comment she could ever make to me. Apparently, I was nothing more to her than a "walk all over mat." She had no respect or feelings for me at all.

That night, I went to bed in tears thinking, *"Oh, God! What have I done? What have I gotten myself into? If I decided to leave now, where would I go? Who would even believe me when I tell them that my 8-year senseless relationship has run its course and now, it's over?"* I'm sure that wouldn't have gone over well at all because many have heard me decree and declare that the relationship was over a million times before, only to discover that I had somehow quietly escaped and hopped a Greyhound bus to go right back into the lions' den. Sure, I had a job, but it didn't pay enough to stay there and take the mental abuse. I knew I was in trouble and needed a way out.

I battled in my mind with moving back to Cincinnati. I knew my son would be happy but would be concerned about me still having contact with her or possibly finding my way back to her somehow, some way.

In the relationship, everything was my fault. She was only concerned about me providing for her and her children. It was not relevant to her that I had to take care of my own son back in Cincinnati. The list of mental abuse was vast.

- I wasn't allowed to have contact with my son, causing him not to trust me or want to see me.
- I wasn't allowed to communicate with my son's mom concerning him for any reason.
- I wasn't allowed to send my son money for school clothes and other necessities.
- My son started to hate me.
- I wasn't allowed to make visits back home.
- Paying my child support was equated to taking food out of her kids' mouths and not taking care of her bills and other personal needs.
- She ridiculed me in front of her children by saying things like my son wasn't mine; he was another man's child.
- She insisted that I get a DNA test to prove to her that my son was, indeed, my son — and if the results came back that he was 99.9% positively mine, she was done! The relationship was over.
- All birthdays, holidays, and other gift-giving occasions were cut off from my son. They were to be spent with her and her kids only. Any gifts bought were to be for her children either from the kids' fathers or me.

❖ I was told in many ways that if I did not comply with her demands, I would be taken to court and the judge would rule in her favor — taking away everything I ever owned.

Church: Choose Me or It!

Church was always rough on Sunday mornings. I was faithful to the ministry and in need of God to do something big in my life. I knew I had a lot of stuff going on, but I wanted a way out so that I could hear from Him clearly. My thoughts were always cluttered with the next awful thing I was going to have to endure from her. I couldn't seem to get focused to save my life. On Sunday mornings, she would hear me getting dressed and would associate that as me being "sneaky" or a "dirty dog," just because I wore a suit. That's right. Me wearing a suit would push her clean over the edge and send her into one of her heated frenzies.

She would ask me, *"Why are you trying to be so quiet while getting dressed? Who are you trying to showboat for? Who are you trying to impress? Who is it that you're going to see: one of your church whores? You're just going to church to be seen so that the women can hear you sing. You're still a whore!"* Her goal was to create an argument that would ultimately lead me to not going to church at all.

Neither one of us were living a lifestyle that was pleasing to God, but my heart was still there in the church. I needed to be around people who could lift me up and not ridicule me for not living the way I was supposed to be living. I'm not justifying my behavior under any circumstance. After all, I was good at accepting sound spiritual criticism, be it good or bad. I was just tired of living foul and knew that I was in serious need of help.

Often, she would hide my car keys and cell phone from me while I was in the shower, causing me to have to find another way to church.

She would often wake me up at 3:00 a.m. to interrogate me about other women's numbers in my cell phone, accusing me by saying they weren't real people. It was all a mind game. It was at the top of my list of the most humiliating things I ever had to go through.

Whenever we attended events or were around her friends, I was her "eye candy." She would tell me that I needed to look up to par and catch up with the latest fashions. That meant what I had in my closet wasn't good enough and didn't meet her satisfaction. She picked out what I wore. It didn't matter if I liked it or not. The goal wasn't to make me feel good about myself; it was about making her look good in front of others. She would always boast about how well I sang, followed by putting me on the spot and instructing me to *"sing a little something."* That was followed up by her telling them how well I performed. You get my point, right? I felt like the scum of the Earth. I would ask her a million times over not to put me on display that way. Every chance she had, she would pull the same stunt.

That behavior would continuously go on until she wanted intimacy. I never could understand the thought behind that… I was good enough to sleep with while being hated at the same time. I was so confused. Everyone around me would tell me that she was no good for me, but in my mind, I thought I could somehow "fix" her. So, I thought that if I just hung in there a little while longer, she would eventually come around.

I guess you can say that *"my misery loved her company."* By no means am I playing the victim here because I, too, did my share of dirt. To get back at her, I cheated on her multiple times. I even thought about dating one of her cousins who turned out to be a wonderful person — better than what I had at home. I even had the audacity to tell her cousin how I felt about her and didn't care if the one at home found out about it.

The truth of the matter is that I just wanted to get away from my abuser. I can say that at that moment, I wanted my cake and eat it, too. I was so desperate to find someone — anyone — who would be willing to love me as I loved them. I needed that void in my life to be filled. I was all over the place, not knowing whether I was coming or going from one second to the next. My sense of direction was virtually nonexistent. Everything around me was being affected in the worst possible way, and I had no way to repair it.

Since I'm being transparent, I might as well tell you this: If Hell weren't a factor, the spirit of suicide would have had me beat. I wanted life as I knew it to end. I had no real reason for living anymore. Life for me had become a joke, with me as the guinea pig being used for the punchline.

I wasn't looking for anyone's sympathy; I was looking for a savior—someone who could discern or see the state I was in and could give me a real sense of direction...not their opinion.

I couldn't go to my family. Who would believe me? I certainly didn't want to be ridiculed because of suicidal tendencies. So, I turned to drinking, smoking weed, pornography, lusting after women, and masturbation to take me away from the reality that life had failed me to the fullest. I had lost my father to death, lost my brothers to the prison system, dealt with mentally-abusive girlfriends, and now, I lost myself and my mind altogether. Everything around me that was connected ended up **LOST**.

If you've never been in that type of situation, I can assure you that I would not wish that cloud on anyone. I truly mean that.

One Saturday night, we had the longest, nastiest, dragged-out fight. We threw the most derogatory remarks at each other with dart-like precision. As the excitement started to die down, I remember her telling me, *"I could have you knocked off at any time if I wanted. All I need to do is make a simple phone call."*

"Wow!" I thought to myself. It was at that very moment when my eyes had finally opened. I believed every word she said. It was time for me to end the relationship.

The Other Side of Me

That night, I went to bed with tears streaming down my face. I laid in the bed thinking to myself, *"What a real mess I have made of my life!"* I was so ashamed of myself and what I had allowed myself to become. Family and friends had given me multiple warnings about my need to end the relationship time and again but in my mind, I thought she and I could grow out of our quarrels and, eventually, my love and desire for her would somehow change her. Boy, was I sadly mistaken!

Wow! Wasn't that a lot to take in from someone who just about laid his entire life out there on the line? My truths are shared with a purpose: to let someone out there know that despite all we go through, God loves us unconditionally. It's not the same as man's love. Man can love you today and leave you tomorrow. No matter what, God will remain in control.

It is essential for us to realize that often, we like to play the "Blame Game." We blame God, Satan, or that individual who you feel has wronged you in some way. It becomes a little sketchy when it comes to having to admit the part that we played in the catastrophic event as well. We may find ourselves tested in the fire, only to realize later that the situations we encountered were from our own doing. It's all good when things seem to be going according to plan, and it's to our benefit, but the second it looks like we've hit turbulence or an uneven plain, we suddenly lose all self-control.

Now, what I'm about to say may throw you for a loop.

Remember I told you at the beginning of this book that I solely believe in calling an "ace an ace and a spade a spade"?

Well, this is one of those moments when I can say that I had to stop and look at this thing for what it truly was. I had to realize it takes two to tango and if I was going to tell it, then I was going to tell it **ALL**. I refuse to allow someone else to tell my story because we all know that when another narrates your story, it's never quite the same. There's always a glitch or pieces missing from the puzzle.

So, what I had discovered in my one-sided relationship was that she only did to me what I had allowed. You see, just like the enemy comes to kill, steal, and destroy, she had attacked those things that could devastatingly keep me from the cross: my sole attachment to her (idolatry) and sex. We both knew that sex was one of my strongest weaknesses, in addition to believing that I couldn't do any better outside of her. It was within those final moments that I began to see just how bad things had gotten. I realized I needed God—not a dead-end relationship.

No Blessing from God.

Before I move on, let me say this: I was doing some research on relationships, seeking information on why a lot of them fail. The Bible considers shacking up the opposite of a legitimate marriage. A legitimate marriage consists of a union between a man and woman who have made a covenant and commitment to one another. Shacking up involves neither. Marriage is a union created by God and is one that God blesses.

According to Examiner.com, a whopping 80% of shacking-up relationships end before marriage or end in divorce after marriage. So, the math says that there's an 80% chance that one of two things will happen: After shacking up, you will not get married, **OR** if you do, you won't remain married to that person. One reason is that there is no commitment when you cohabitate before marriage. A relationship without a commitment will not last, and marriage is the biggest commitment you can make in life.

That was *"The Other Side of Me."* It was the layout of my life. I wanted to be connected to someone for the sake of having someone there in my life, even if it meant losing m life in the process. I had allowed my self-worth, dignity, character, and integrity to be stripped away. I wanted the void to be filled—not fixed.

Oh! Another thing I've learned in the process is that Jesus Christ is, in fact, the **ONLY ONE** who can fill the void. He is, indeed, a Heart-Fixer and Mind-Regulator.

When we finally understand we can do nothing without God, He will begin to remove things out of our lives that were never intended to be there—be it people or things. Of course, there are things He will allow to happen for our good and His glory.

The passage of scripture that speaks volumes to our circumstances is Galatians 5:7:

> *"Ye did run well; who did hinder you that ye should not obey the truth?"*

The scripture asks the question: What or who did you allow to knock you off-course when you were already on the right path? I recommend doing a self-assessment or self-awareness check to see where you stand naturally and spiritually. In doing that, it allows you to check your motives, character, feelings, and desires for why you do the things that you do. In retrospect, you should want to see if those things line up with the will of God for your life.

I am at the point in my life where everything I do has serious consequences attached to them because I have so much to lose. I can strongly relate to the song that says, *"I've been through too much not to worship Him."*

If you know it was God who brought you out of the crack house, out of that adulterated lifestyle that was leading you into the clinching arms of HIV, porn websites, the local neighborhood man/woman who sells himself/herself because that's where they feel their very best, you ought to tell God **"THANK YOU!"**

It is a fact that many have not made it out of some of the things mentioned above. The truth is that everyone won't make it out because there are times when God allows certain things to happen in our lives to make us stronger. Again, it is imperative that we understand that for everything, there is a season and a time to every purpose under Heaven. Ecclesiastes 3:5-6 tells us that there is *"a time to cast away stones, and a time to gather stones together; a time to embrace, and a time to refrain from embracing; a time to get, and a time to lose; a time to keep, and a time to cast away."*

The Other Side of Me

So, understand that everything won't always be peaches and cream. Now and then, our feathers will get ruffled a little bit, only to realize that this, too, shall pass. That's when we begin to look at where we are today and see how far God has brought us out. Many of you owe God the best praise you can muster up. Were it not for His extended grace and mercy on your life, you might have already received a glimpse of where you would be: somewhere in the crack house, another labeled tag in the morgue that the streets claimed, a person with a mental health condition in a state hospital, or behind bars. That's why when your feet hit the floor every morning, and you have breath in your body, you ought to tell God about how grateful you are.

If He saved your daughter from becoming another teenaged mother, you ought to tell God **"THANK YOU!"**

If the job laid you off and the bills seem like they won't stop piling up but they're getting paid, you ought to tell God **"THANK YOU!"**

If you just dodged that accident that would have claimed your life if you were "there" a mere eight seconds earlier, you ought to tell God **"THANK YOU!"**

If He saved your son from becoming strung out, or he dodged that bullet, then you ought to put this book down right now, lift your hands high, and give God the loudest **"SHABACH PRAISE"** your voice can handle because you have the good sense to know that without Him, it wouldn't have been done.

My friend, we serve an Almighty God who cannot fail. One thing that we can **ALL** attest to with surety is that *"He may not come when we want Him, but He'll be there right on time. He's an on-time God... Yes, He is!"* Saints of God, I can't stress it enough: Learn and know who you are in God so that you'll know how to fight when the enemy tries to come up against you.

The Bible says, *"My people perish for lack of knowledge"* (Hosea 4:6). Let's look at that scripture a little closer to get a better understanding of what God is saying.

At the time, Israel was missing something. Scripture talks about "rejected knowledge" that is parallel to "forgotten the law." Israel failed to acknowledge the **LORD** as their God (see Hosea 4:1). The people did not simply lack knowledge; they actively rejected Him. In return, God would reject them as well as "forget" their children (He would remove His future blessing from the nation).

What were the terms of God's covenant with ancient Israel?

> *"Now, therefore, if you will indeed obey My voice*
> *and keep My covenant, then you shall be a special treasure*
> *to Me above all people..."*
> **(Exodus 19:5)**

> *"Then all the people answered together and said,*
> *'All that the Lord has spoken, we will do.'"*
> **(Exodus 19:8)**

The future blessing would be that if they obeyed, God promised to make of them a great nation and to protect, prosper, and provide for them.

What did God say would happen if the Israelites failed to live up to their obligations under the covenant?

"But if you will not listen to Me and carry out all these commands, and if you reject My decrees and abhor My laws and fail to carry out all My commands, and so violate My covenant, I will bring upon you sudden terror, wasting diseases, and fever that will destroy your sight and drain away your life. You will plant seeds in vain because your enemies will eat it. I will set My face against you so that you will be defeated by your enemies; those who hate you will rule over you, and you will flee, even when no one is pursuing you.
If, after all this, you will not listen to Me,
I will punish you for your sins seven times over."
(Leviticus 26:14-18)

As with the covenant God made with Abraham, the covenant He made with Israel contained conditions, duties, and obligations. The people's acceptance of those conditions cemented their relationship with God, but their later disobedience cut them off from the blessings God had promised.

How and why did the Israelites fail to fulfill their obligations under the covenant?

> *"They did not keep the covenant of God;*
> *they refused to walk in His law and forgot His works*
> *and His wonders that He had shown them."*
> **(Psalm 78:10-11)**

So, if God would do all of that for Israel, how much more would He do for us? If we would simply keep His commandments and do His will, then He'll take care of us. His Word says, *"Delight yourself also in the LORD, and He shall give you the desires of your heart"* (Psalm 37:4).

God wants to change the way you perceive things. He wants to change your heart and mind, but you must first want change to take place in your life. Remember: He will not force Himself upon us; He gives us free will to make a **CHOICE**.

Chapter Fourteen

The Day I Served the Devil His Walking Papers

Sunday morning came, and I was up early to get ready for church. There was a burning desire in my spirit to get there and give my life to Jesus Christ.

The service was awesome as usual. Praise and worship were heavy in the Lord's house, and the atmosphere was conducive for a mighty move of God. I found myself harboring a sense of urgency to get to the altar—while the pastor was preaching. For my own selfish reasons, I was hoping that he would hurry up and finish his sermon because all I wanted to do was get to the altar to accomplish the task I had set out to do early on in my day.

As the pastor was ending his sermon, he asked (as one with genuine concern for his people), *"Is there one?"* Instantly, I locked eyes with one of my dearest friends in Christ, Evangelist Joyce Bryant, as she stood at the altar beckoning for me to come. She knew that I needed something. She knew of the horrible relationship I was in. She knew I was in desperate need of God and knew I wanted Him. She knew I was ready to receive Him at that very moment. She spoke to me as if she had known me all my life and said to me, *"I have heard the voice of the Lord,*

*Brother Keith. You need to change your life today. God is not pleased with your living arrangements and sinful nature. God said, "Choose ye **THIS DAY** whom you will serve, for I have extended my grace and mercy for far too long."*

I don't think I've ever been surer of myself that nothing or no one was going to stop me from going forward. I lifted my hands and received Christ back into my life right then and there. Before the end of the service, I served the devil his walking papers and ended my 8-year, one-sided relationship. That was a major weight lifted off of my shoulders. I left the church feeling empowered and ready to move on with my life with **GOD** in it.

Even though we rode together in the same car, she could see how anxious I had become to move on to the next level in God and that it was going to be imperative that I rode this thing out. The relationship had finally ended.

Soon after, I moved out of her house and into a 3-bedroom home of my own. For a while, I stayed single and worked on improving my relationship with God. I had gotten used to being on my own and back active in the ministry. I made the conscious decision to not date for a while. I wanted to get myself together and try to restore the faltering relationship with my son. It took some time to regain his trust and forgiveness after the unsettling rollercoaster ride I had taken him on all of those years. I made up my mind that no one would **EVER** come before him ever again. I wasn't willing to destroy what had been rebuilt between us.

The Other Side of Me

Sometime after that, I reconnected with my high school sweetheart. We dated for about a year and a half and shortly after that, became one on May 4, 2013. I am forever grateful for our sons, Michael and Adrian, and for God showing me what true love is.

I had come ready to receive what God had in store for me and again, my friend; He wants to do the same for you. If you will, do a quick recap of your life right now at this very moment.

Pause...

Now, be completely honest with yourself. Are you living up to your highest potential in God? I would venture to say that none of us are, yet we're striving to be Christ-like daily. Right? Isn't it great to know that you have an Almighty, All-Powerful, and All-Knowing God who loves you unconditionally and only wants the very best for you that He would lay down His life for you to give **YOU** an expected end? That's the type of God we serve. We serve a God who extends His grace and mercy to us daily in hopes that we would see just how great He is.

Although none of us are deserving of it, God is merciful to even the worst offenders, sinners, and law-breakers. Even though He knows our guilt, He doesn't always issue the punishment deserved. Romans 3:23-24 says, "*...all have sinned and fall short of the glory of God and are justified freely by His grace; through His mercy and grace, He provided a way for our sins to be forgiven through our acceptance of Christ Jesus*" — even though we don't deserve it. Coupled with grace (being given God's gift of forgiveness, though we've done nothing to deserve it), mercy is shown because He loves us and only asks that we accept His Son by faith.

So, again: What will it take for you to realize how much you need God in your life? If we start with forgiving ourselves first of any wrongdoings to ourselves (or others, for that matter), that is a great start! Acknowledging that you have issues and making up your mind that you must get that "thing" right with your brother or sister is a sure way of getting to the very heart of God.

If there are issues that you need to get right with family, then now is the time to do it. As you see, many people are leaving the face of this Earth without a moment's notice. They are here today and gone tomorrow. No one is promised the next minute, and there is nothing or no one that you should allow to separate you from the love of Christ.

My life's experiences were necessary for me to see that God had me in the palm of His hands all that time. It was frustrating many times to go through what I endured because it was hard for me to understand what He was doing in my life. It is sometimes hard to stretch out on faith when you can't see what the results are going to be in the end. I have learned that it is at that moment when we must draw nearer to God all the more and wait it out. Patience and trust in God are essential in the Christian walk. Without them, how do you expect God to move when you've tied His hands with doubt and unbelief?

The Other Side of Me

I challenge you today to seek God's face. Find out who you are in Him (if you haven't already). I know it's a daily process, but you would be surprised to find out things you didn't know about yourself and God. He wants to commune with you. He wants you to tell Him all about your struggles, desires, hopes, and dreams — and vice-versa. He wants to share many things with you that you didn't know about yourself and Him as well. Remember: He created you, so He knows **ALL** things and He knows **ALL** about you. There is nothing new under the sun to Him. He created it **ALL** — the sun, the moon, the stars, the universe…*and YOU.*

If ever there were a time when we needed Him the most, we need Him now with the way the world is today. The Bible says in 2 Timothy 3:2, *"For men shall be lovers of their own selves, covetous, boasters, proud, blasphemers, disobedient to parents, unthankful, unholy."* The Apostle Paul forewarns Timothy what the last days would be like, with the reasons why making us wise unto salvation and aware that we will be the best antidote against the corruptions of the times we live in. Therefore, we are encouraged to hold on even more to our integrity and salvation because of the world's sinful nature. We are, in fact, living in the End Times (the last days).

We (the saints of God) should know by now that there has been a significant shift in the land in which we live today. Never in a million years would I have thought I would bear witness to shootings and killings in our school systems and churches. Now, we have security services in place in just about every sector across America.

And then, there is a reversed role in the parent/child dynamic. Children are now in control and placing high demands on the parents by way of the media and video games. There is also an extraordinary amount of men missing from the home—leaving our young men to try sorting out the pieces of their lives and their daughters seeking unfulfilled love from a man in the streets rather than being taught how to be properly loved, cherished, and respected by **ALL** men. By no means am I dismissing the mother; she is, by far, often the nurturer.

Just as the mothers should be grooming their daughters to be young, respectable ladies, we must remember that these girls are modeling after what they see. So, if mommy is one who brings home an "Uncle" with a different name every other night, you can rest assured that her daughter will either pick up on some of those same habits or become a potential predatory victim at an early age, either by the mother's boyfriend or even sometimes by the husband in the home. Ultimately, this unstable environment usually causes our children to act out and vent fearful and painful emotions as silent cries for help.

Men and women have reversed roles in their sexuality, only to call it "God's will" for their lives. The Bible clearly speaks against the union of same-sex marriages. I didn't write the Bible, but many will argue or challenge this issue because they don't want to be called into question about their own lifestyle. They simply want to live it out and whatever comes with that, so be it! *"It is what it is!"* is what they say…

What has happened to our government officials? Have they become a part of the criminal lineup of predatorial sexual scandals in our media and White House? Every other day seems to bring one to light, with very little remorse and compassion after being revealed. Those high-profile proteges are being televised in our homes right in our faces! Yes, this is supposed to be the "land of the free and the home of the brave," but I am reminded that whom the **SON** sets free is free, indeed. David said to his son Solomon, *"Be strong and courageous and do it. Do not be afraid and do not be dismayed, for the LORD God, even my God is with you. He will not leave you or forsake you, until all the work for the service of the house of the LORD is finished."*

There was a time when families could come together, sit down, and watch a good, wholesome family TV sitcom. Now, it's all about the ratings and who can stir up the most ruckus. Folks, what has happened to us as a nation? Why do we no longer value each other and stand on the principles of what's right and wrong?

Let me stop there.

By no means and I passing judgment on anyone. I realize that we all must sweep around our own front door. Still, I am unapologetic for my stand because I am speaking on matters that we know to be the truth. Now, I'm sure I will get some *"AMENS!"* and even some frowns, but that's okay. Either way you and I look at it, we will eventually have to answer as individuals for the choices we make down here on Earth.

We must repent and get back to our first love — Jesus Christ. We must get back to the place where God has called us to *"come out from amongst them [the world] and be ye separated"* (Romans 12:2).

"Therefore, if any man be in Christ, he is a new creature: old things are passed away; behold, all things are become new in Him."
(2 Corinthians 5:17, KJV)

That means if you have been saved and have received God's love:

- Life can't separate you from it.
- Death can't separate you from it.
- Even demons can't separate you from it.
- The past, present, and future can't separate you from it.
- Absolutely **NOTHING** will be able to separate you from it.

We must recognize the fact that Jesus is soon to return, and He's coming back for a church (His Bride) that's without a spot, wrinkle, or any blemishes (see Ephesians 5:27).

I can assure you that I am no better than the next person. Trust me when I say that. I will be the first to stand and say that all the dirt and cobwebs have not been removed entirely from my closet. God is still working on me. I'm allowing Him to do what He needs in my life, as I hope the very same for you. I have a strong love for all people and want to see **US** do better and make it into the Kingdom of Heaven together.

In Philippians 2:12, Paul wrote, *"Work out your own salvation with fear and trembling."* Does that mean we stop witnessing to the lost? No. How can we—as saints of God—say that we serve an Almighty God and risen Savior, but never share with others who He is? So, what does it mean to "work out our own salvation"? In this instance, Paul was saying that it's not enough for us to keep this great gospel to ourselves; it is vital that we strive to be unified and on one accord, bringing the lost aboard so that Jesus Christ can do the saving of their souls. It is solely our job to share the gospel (the Good News) of Jesus Christ, and we can't do that if we don't have a committed relationship with Him.

So, in other words, salvation is not worked out in our lives because it has not been completed in us until we are of one mind and spirit with our brothers and sisters in Christ. When there is *"grumbling and disputing"* (Philippians 2:14) in the church, that's when we need to be admonished to work out our salvation. It's also when we need to be reminded that *"if there is any encouragement in Christ, then be of the same mind"* (Philippians 2:1-2).

I am quite saddened to see that our world has become what it is today, yet I am confident in knowing that Jesus Christ has the final say—no matter what. I urge each of you reading this book to take a serious look at where you are today and ask yourself, *"Am I truly walking and living according to God's perfect plan for my life? Am I living up to my fullest potential? Or am I straddling the fence with one foot in the church and the other outside the door—wanting to be a better person, but unsure of how to separate the two? Am I making an impact or am I a hindrance to the body of Christ?"*

So, now that you've answered those questions, where do you go from here? I'm glad you asked!

Jesus said, *"If anyone would come after Me, he must deny himself and take up his cross daily and follow Me"* (Luke 9:23).

Fast every day, and you'll be just like Jesus.

I want to extend a special thanks to Evangelist Joyce Bryant for how she helped shape my life for the better. I am forever indebted to her for the love she has shown my wife and me. I know that I have a true friend and big sister in Christ who pulls no punches and accepts no excuses when it comes to ministry and serving Christ. She's one who knows how to give you that stern look and soft voice when she says, *"I love you, but I won't baby you! It's either Heaven or Hell. Who will you serve? Choose ye this day! Get it right!"* I love her for that. Never has she made me feel uncomfortable in my sinful state. She would simply tell me about God's love, and I could take it for what it was worth or leave it.

My pastor was a no-nonsense man who knew how to get you good while holding a smile on his face that made you want to live right. In fact, you weren't going to operate in ministry under him with a messy spirit. From the front door to the altar, you had to have the heart to live right or sit down until you developed one. He taught me how to have character and integrity under his ministry and the importance of upright living.

Today, I carry those attributes not only in ministry where I serve but in my daily affairs. For that very reason, I say, **"THANK YOU, Pastor Phillip L. McPheeters.** *You are an amazing man of God, and I will forever remain humbled and honored to have served under such a great pastor who gave me and the other deacons a platform to grow in God."*

****

Temptation is a desire to engage in short-term urges for enjoyment that threatens long-term goals. In the context of some religions, temptation is the inclination to sin.

Think for just a moment about the comic book series and movie "Superman: The Man of Steel." His nemesis, Lex Luthor, always tried to bring down Superman with the one thing that could kill him: the element kryptonite. It was Superman's ultimate weakness.

What does it mean for someone to be **YOUR** kryptonite?

In plain speak, it means that the person or object referred to, for some reason, makes one lose one's resolve, rendering a person easily influenced or coerced to doing something they're usually not predisposed to doing. In other words, kryptonite (in this context) is a metaphor for "weakness."

That is how Satan uses his tactics to come after God's people. He uses the very thing that can bring harm to us and our relationship with our Heavenly Father.

Much like our adversary (the fallen angel; Lucifer; Satan), he wanted Jesus to bow down and release all power to him. Lex Luthor wanted to kill Superman, as he feared that a man as powerful as Superman would one day become a dictator of sorts, using his "godlike" powers to take over the world. God's ultimate purpose for dying on the cross for our sins would be that we would spend eternal life with Him according to John 3:16:

"For God so loved the world, that He gave His Only Begotten Son; that whosoever believeth in Him should not perish, but have everlasting life."

So, what does it all mean? It means that even ***Jesus*** was tempted by Satan. Matthew 4:1-11 (KJV) reads as follows:

"Then Jesus was led up by the Spirit into the wilderness to be tempted by the devil. And when He had fasted forty days and forty nights, afterward He was hungry. Now, when the tempter came to Him, he said, 'If you are the Son of God, command that these stones become bread.' But He answered and said, 'It is written, 'Man shall not live by bread alone, but by every word that proceeds from the mouth of God.' Then the devil took Him up into the holy city, set Him on the pinnacle of the temple, and said to Him, 'If you are the Son of God, throw yourself down. For it is written: 'He shall give His angels charge over you' and 'In their hands, they shall bear you up, lest you dash your foot against a stone.' Jesus said to him, 'It is written again, 'You shall not tempt the LORD your God.' Again, the devil took Him up on an exceeding high mountain and showed Him all the kingdoms of the world and their glory. And he said to Him, 'All these things I will give you if you will fall down and worship me.' Then Jesus said to him, 'Away with you, Satan! For it is written, 'You shall worship

the LORD your God, and Him only you shall serve.' Then the devil left Him and, behold, angels came and ministered to Him."

The moral of the story is: For Christ to fall and worship Satan would have been to acknowledge the devil's lordship over Him.

Are you allowing someone or things to take precedence over your life? If you can honestly admit to that by answering yes, then half of your battle has been won. You must never allow the fleshly part of your life to take precedence over your spiritual life. Set your mind on the things of God and don't allow anything or anyone to deter you from that.

"Set your affection on things above, not on things on the Earth."
(Colossians 3:2)

Chapter Fifteen

The Demonic Suicide Attack

There was nothing or no one I could turn to so, in my mind, suicide was my only option. I recall the night so clearly as if it was just last night…

My girlfriend and I were laying on the bedroom floor talking about bills and other matters. There was a nasty, raging storm going on outside and then suddenly, out of nowhere, I became enraged. It was like a demonic force had been lying dormant in me, waiting to make its appearance at just the right moment.

I started yelling at her and demanding that she leave my apartment at once. I stood up, went into the living room, and stood near the corner of the wall. I had no furniture in my apartment except for an old flower-print couch my sister, Rene, had given me. I remember telling my girlfriend that I was tired of struggling, tired of people lying and taking advantage of me, and tired of her always nagging me about her needs and desires. I stood looking at the old, stained bay windows as I entertained the thought of jumping out of it and ending it all.

She cried, begged, and pleaded with me not to do it. She didn't want to have to live with that night on her conscious for the rest of her life. After maybe two hours of trying to calm me down, she finally went home. We ended up talking more that night and decided we'd take a break from each other. About a week later, she called to let me know that she was calling it quits because of my baggage. It was much more than what she could deal with, so she and I ended the relationship and went our separate ways—never to see each other again.

To me, she had become the judge, juror, and executioner. She had thrown me into this "mental prison" and threw away the key. We would see each other in passing, and I would often ask one of our mutual friends about her. However, when she saw me, she would quickly turn and go in the opposite direction, just to avoid the possibility of eye contact with me.

I can admit today that I was a bag of nuts. I prided myself on my life's failures, not knowing that everyone wasn't going to join me on my "woe is me boat." The bottom line is this: I wasn't stable enough in the mind to be in a committed relationship. She had way too many dreams and aspirations, and I was a major setback to her progress in a lot of ways.

THE TRUTH HURT: Evangelist Joyce Bryant & Pastor Phillip L. McPheeters

The truth hurts, but these things needed to be said. It was time-out for sweeping all of those generational curses under the rug. When were things ever going to come to light? When were we ever going to get clarity and healing from all of the undercover lies?

I had such a thirst to get to the altar because I knew that I would be able to break free of the chains of bondage that captivated me. I knew I would find healing, deliverance, safety, and rest in Christ.

> *"...if only I could touch the hem of His garment, then I know I will be made whole."*
> **(Luke 8:43-48)**

Family Ties: My Reality Outlook

For me, I just wanted to address the elephant in the room. I grew up not having a close relationship with my parents because they worked a lot to provide for us the best way they knew how. Still, I would've liked to have known what it was like to go to a football game, basketball game, or even fishing with my father. My mother was a lover of puzzles, word and connect-the-dot games, and clothes shopping (she called it "eye buying") in her spare time. So, I never really knew what their likes and dislikes were.

Still, we were a close-knit family of 13 siblings who had a strong love connection for each other but pretty much did our own thing. We were a well-known and well-liked family in our community. Our love for each other was like no other. That's something we can all brag on, and we still have that closeness to this very day.

My enemies consisted of the neighborhood bullies (who bullied everyone they could) at most. Who didn't have those in their life?

The Other Side of Me

All while growing up, I found myself extremely bitter because of all the past adverse events that had transpired in my life. It appears the negatives far outweighed the positives (that's what I recall most from my childhood). Although I never talked about my past to anyone other than my wife, I was 99.9% sure that not too many people wanted to hear a sob story about the setbacks of my life. Today, most preachers would tell me, "Stop harping on your past relationships and just move on. You're not the only one who's experienced hurt in your life; we all have in one way or another." I couldn't agree more. However, I'm reminded that it is our past hurts and failures that are there to build us up. That's why they're called "life lessons."

If we didn't go through things, how would we be able to relate to one another if we couldn't give some sort of sound feedback to their situation? I don't dispute that we all handle life's complicated rollercoaster differently. I also understand that these setbacks are teaching moments for our own growth. Therefore, we should be learning from them and moving ahead in life. Sometimes, I wonder if speaking out about our past creates barriers for those who are going through their storms...

What's the right and wrong message to relay if we're supposed to be ministering to the lost? I know that it is Jesus Christ who does the saving, but what role do I play when the lost soul is experiencing some of the same storms I've already faced? What do I tell them? Do I say, **"Stop being a cry baby, deal with that mountain (giant), and move on"**?

For so long, we have swept our issues under the rug because we were told to "get over it." Many of our problems have gone undealt with because we turned a deaf ear to others' situations, leaving them to cope with whatever the outcome may be. I always try to keep in mind that it is only by God's grace and mercy that I've been sustained this far and that the only reason why I am still here is because of His love and compassion for me. It's not because I've done anything so great; its because He unconditionally loved me, despite my faults and response to life's tumultuous moments.

So, what happens when the tables are turned, and you're now the one in need of this same compassion? Are you trying to "just get over it"? Or are you reaching out in need of a lending ear—someone who is willing to listen…not talk or give an opinionated response? Think about it: Not everyone is looking for sympathy. Empathy, however, is helpful now and then. I'm not speaking ill against spiritual leaders or the body of Christ in general. I'm trying to get clarification on how we should handle our emotions besides running to God all the time for every little obstacle that comes our way.

Now, I will admit that not all of my days were bad. A lot of them were actually great! What continued to play in the back of my mind were the scars that plagued me. Sure, my mother introduced my siblings and me to Jesus Christ, but after that, I had no real positive experiences that I could compare in that sense. I wanted to remember the positive things about my upbringing more than anything, but all I could see was the struggle.

The Other Side of Me

I couldn't seem to understand why my mom had this thing about not wanting to participate in parts of the church service. She wanted to come in, sit down in the back pews, and be seen—not heard. If the Sunday School teacher asked her a question, she would speak in a very low voice where she could barely be heard. Why did she act that way?

For whatever the reason, she wanted her children to be vocal. I think she wanted us to be able to say what she was afraid to say or didn't want to say. She never liked speaking in front of others or being put on the spot. She wanted us to answer some of the questions during the Sunday School lesson, though. It was always her "thing" to compliment the women in the church on their attire, followed by her saying, *"See, if I had that kind of money, those are the types of clothes I'd wear."* It was like she wished she could be like them.

I want to point out that I love my mother dearly. I truly believe her heart was in the right place in many instances. I also think that life's circumstances robbed her of her ability to get beyond her own childhood/teenage issues that ultimately caused her own children's needs to suffer.

If I had a dollar for every time I cried because we had to do without, I'd be a rich man right now—literally! I know very well what it's like to be in lack and not know where the next meal was coming from or how the bills were going to get paid. How about needing $5.00 to put in the gas tank while wondering if God will ever answer that prayer? Those circumstances may prompt the following questions: Is God really real? Does He play the "Favoritism Game"? Or perhaps being saved is only for the "chosen" ones.

Have you ever thought, *"I guess I'm not good enough"* or *"I guess I'll just have to get whatever I need the best way I know how!"*

I don't want to sound like I was trying to 'guilt trip' God, but again, that was my reality.

I didn't know much about how to pray or how to cry out to God. I thought it was just way too much work. I felt like a dog being taunted by its master with a treat. I wasn't about to do tricks for treats just to get something from God. Little did I know that He was testing me to see how I would weather the storm, only to find myself repeating the same thing…

We are constantly being tested because God is trying to get us to trust Him more and more. We must realize that man is not our source; God is. What He has given, He can also take away.

"Trust in the LORD and do good; dwell in the land and enjoy safe pasture. Delight yourself in the LORD, and He will give you the desires of your heart."
(Psalm 37:3-4)

"Commit your way to the LORD; trust in Him, and He will do this: He will make your righteousness shine like the dawn, the justice of your cause like the noonday sun. Be still before the LORD and wait patiently for Him."
(Psalm 37:5-7a)

The Other Side of Me

God is a rewarder of them that diligently seek Him.

It was hard for me to trust God because I couldn't see Him working it out on my behalf. I couldn't see the light at the end of the tunnel. It wasn't enough for me to see and hear others speak of how good He was to them when there I was, struggling to stay afloat. I started believing that it was meant for me to be alone; to try to put the pieces of life's puzzle together on my own so that it would all make sense to me.

I am now 50 years old and still haven't figured out this thing called "life." Nevertheless, I am so glad that I now know Him as my personal Lord and Savior. He is my Way-Maker out of no way, my Healer and Deliverer, my King of kings and Lord of lords. In Him, I am made strong. In Him, I am made whole. I am the apple of His eye. I am the head and not the tail. I am above and not beneath. I am who God says I am. I am fearfully and wonderfully made. I was created in His image. I was created for His purpose. I was created to serve Him. I was created to worship Him.

> *"God is a Spirit: and they that worship Him must worship Him in spirit and in truth."*
> **(John 4:24, KJV)**

I had to ask God to forgive me for not believing that He could meet my needs. I was one of those who believed in "instant gratification." I needed to have my needs met right then and there until I had to own up to the fact that God doesn't come when we want Him to, but He's always right on time. I never considered myself an Atheist because I didn't know what one was in the beginning. I simply didn't know who God was. I didn't understand His power and what it could do in my life.

I started reminiscing over how I didn't have much as a child—and didn't see myself having much as an adult. I could see others being blessed all around me but couldn't see myself in the same light. I battled with Hebrews 11:1:

> *"Now, faith is the substance of things hoped for,
> the evidence of things not seen."*

This put a real strain on the word "trust" for me. It was like asking me to put all my eggs into one basket, only to be disappointed in the end. I wanted to believe God, though; I just didn't know **HOW**. For me, I always found it difficult to put my trust in Him because:

1. I didn't understand the power of prayer.
2. I didn't understand that trust is our lifeline to God.
3. It became tiresome as I attempted to do it.
4. It became repetitious and boring.
5. It was a waste of time and energy.
6. I was afraid of receiving confirmation to an answer that I didn't want to hear.
7. The waiting process seemed way too long.

Prayer Statistics

According to Cathe Laurie (2012), the three top reasons why people don't pray are:

1. We don't think we have time.
2. We don't think it is important.
3. We don't believe it makes any difference.

First, we DO have the time! According to a recent article in *The Wall Street Journal*, a Neilson study reported that in 2010, Americans spent 63.5 billion minutes on social networks. Another Neilson study indicated that an average Internet user spends 68 hours on the Internet per month — about 2 hours and 6 minutes per day. So, these studies prove that we do have the time…we're just not using it wisely.

Secondly, prayer is necessary! While on Earth, Jesus was dependent on spending vital time in prayer with the Father. How much more should we? Hebrews 5:7 reveals the passionate prayer life of our Lord. During the days of Jesus' life on Earth, He offered up prayers and petitions with loud cries and tears to the One who could save Him from death, and He was heard because of His reverent submission.

Before you think you don't need time to pray, think of the staggering defeat of the Israelite army when they fought against the little city called "Ai." Confident with the victory over the mighty fortress of Jericho, they neglected to pray and consult the Lord before going into battle. Bold and careless, they were soundly defeated.

Lastly, prayer does make a difference! Prayer is *"not for getting man's will done in Heaven, but for getting God's will done on Earth."* Remember that our Father is in Heaven and we are on the Earth. But as His children, we can be confident that He wants to bless, use, guide, and provide for us. Perhaps "you have not because you ask not."

> *"Pray without ceasing."*
> **(1 Thessalonians 5:17)**

Everyone goes to God for different reasons. My needs may not be your needs. We may not share the same desires. One thing we can all agree on is that without prayer, we won't get the answers we need to our problems.

There's a passage of scripture that states *"we [sometimes] do not know what we ought to pray for"* (Romans 8:26). Not knowing what to do in prayer is one of the main reasons people don't pray. So, in a lot of instances, we'd rather try working out the situation on our own or simply wait it out to see what the outcome may be — be it positive or negative.

For me, life has been like a rollercoaster of events that never stops. I longed to know what it felt like to have balance. There's nothing wrong with issues that come to challenge our faith, but when it seems like you can **NEVER** pass the test and find yourself faced with that same challenge, one's thought may be, **"Lord, when in the world is this going to be over with?"**

The Other Side of Me

"Count it all joy, my brothers, when you meet trials of various kinds, for you know that the testing of your faith produces steadfastness. And let steadfastness have its full effect, that you may be perfect and complete, lacking in nothing."
(James 1:2-4)

Chapter Sixteen

Distractions

I found myself faced with many distractions that came from poor relationship choices and the people I surrounded myself with. When it comes to you and God, sometimes you must become selfish in how you spend your time. You see, a lot of times, the people around you don't want to see you succeed; they would rather you fail.

Often, when people see that you're attempting to make a change for the better, they will sometimes associate you as being an "arrogant pompous" — one who is described as behaving or speaking in a very serious way because they think they are more important than they are. When you do a self-assessment, you will most likely find that it is a great tool to use in helping you map out some of the positives and extract the negatives to become a better person.

We can all stand to improve the quality of our lives, right? Even in that, those in your space will try to convince others to give you the cold shoulder without just-cause. They will talk about you when they recognize there is a calling that has been assigned to your life. To put it plainly, they don't understand your walk with God.

The Other Side of Me

The truth remains that people are going to be who they are. That's what makes the world go around. They talked about Jesus! Just like they talked about Him, you can rest assured that they'll be coming for you, too. You can bet your bottom dollar that you won't be the last person on their radar whom they sense has joined the "Goody Two-Shoes" train.

The other truth of the matter is that you're not going to be able to please everyone, no matter how hard you try. So, there's no sense in trying and losing sleep over those who apparently don't have your best interests at heart. If you value any amount of anointing you may think you have left, then you better guard it with every inch of your life. You have way too much to lose. Don't throw it away for a bunch of opinionated people with no hope or drive for destiny.

You must know who you are in Christ. You must know that it is He who created you and not you yourself. He gave you life. It is He who birthed you with purpose. You must rise above your haters and move forward in what God's plan is for your life, or else you'll eventually become part of the "rich graveyard."

The 'rich graveyard' is where a lot of people have died with unfulfilled purposes and dreams. Now, do you want to become one of those people? There is nothing more devastating to man than dying with all of that wasted potential locked up and it not be birthed into something great. What are you waiting for? Start that business. Write that book. Finish school. The bottom line is this: Don't let others abort what God has put down on the inside of you. Let it out!

There is someone right now waiting on you to move in your calling that God has given you so that they can break free and get what God has for them. But because you are still stuck waiting on everyone else's approval for what you know God has called you to do, you will eventually miss what God is trying to do in your life. We — me included — have to learn how to get past people's opinions and do what saith the **LORD**.

It is God who gives the increase, not man. So, again: What are you waiting on to do what He has told you to do?

For years, I lived a life of fear. I worried about the opinions of family members, friends, and church folk, only to find out that God was the only one who gives and takes away. He's the one who gives the increase. I didn't understand that He was my source; not man. I feared being laughed at and told that my vision wouldn't work. I saw a life full of empty promises, regrets, and "should've - could've - would'ves." I vowed that this would not be the legacy I leave to my kids or the next generation. I owe it to my God and myself to live a life that's pleasing and most fulfilling to Him. I refuse to leave this Earth having never reached my destiny because I listened to others. To me, there is no excuse.

So, with having said all of that…

Try bonding with people who are going somewhere in life — those who can pour knowledge and wisdom into your vision. Connect with those who don't want what you have but are willing to help you get whatever it is that you need to get ahead. Stop linking up with people who can't give you sound advice but feel their personal opinions should carry weight in your vision and circumstances.

Listen: You don't owe man an explanation. Only what you do for Christ will last. He should be the only one you should consult unless He decides to place someone in your path who can give you sound advice. God wants the best for us all. He wants us to have the best that life has to offer from both a natural and spiritual perspective. Most importantly, He wants a **"YES!"** from us—a *"YES!"* to His will and a *"YES!"* to His way. (We know that in everything, God works for the good of those who love Him and are called to His purpose (Romans 8:28).)

God makes it very clear to us that He knows exactly what our needs are.

> *"'For I know the thoughts I think toward you,' says the LORD, 'thoughts of peace, and not of evil, to give you an expected end.'"*
> **(Jeremiah 29:11)**

In that passage, He's giving us a promise that there is hope in our future that the history of our people is not yet over; the "hope" is that there is a better time in store for us. In Him, we can rest assured that our "expected end" (the future) will result in something great if we stand on His promises.

> *"And let us not be weary in well-doing; for in due season, we shall reap if we faint not."*
> **(Galatians 6:9)**

In that passage, we find that the Christian life is a marathon race. The race is not given to the swift nor the strong, but to the one who endures to the end. We're not doing His good work to get accolades and a pat on the back, but rather to live out the plan He has for our lives.

So, what will it take for you to yield to God's Word? What will it take to change your heart?

It wasn't until I had my first actual encounter with God that I was able to see who He really was in my life. He started showing me that there was so much more to Him than just a *"Thank you, Jesus."* He began to show me that He was God — the Heart-Fixer, the Mind-Regulator, a Friend to the friendless, and a Father to the fatherless wrapped up all in one. He is so much more than we can even fathom. What a mighty God we serve!

You see, I had to get to the place in God where I could trust Him to fix my life totally without expecting my past hurts and failures to repair themselves. I just needed to get to the place in God where I could steal away to get to know and hear from Him without any distractions from other people and things in my ear. I knew that if I was going to get any answers from God, I was going to have to step out on faith and shut down the opinions of others and their thoughts as to what they believed God was saying in **MY** life. We sometimes look for validation in people to do what we want to do because we don't want to do what's right. So, if someone's willing to jump on the bandwagon with us, that's pretty much all we need to be within our own right to carry out whatever it is that we want to do, whether it be right or wrong. Somewhere along the way, we want to be justified in our own actions, only to return and play that old "Blame Game" if things don't quite pan out the way we intended. The last thing we want to hear is, *"I told you so!"* when the plan fails.

God was showing me that through all the battle scars, letdowns, rollercoaster rides, and roadblocks in my life that He had never left my side. He was there all the time. Much like the Prodigal Son who squandered all of his fortune, only to return home after realizing it was probably in his best interest to do so, I concluded that I needed my Heavenly Father the most.

Jesus, being the Great, Almighty God that He is, saw that His son (me) had returned home, was in need, and welcomed him back with open arms and a feast. He knew before I even left Toledo at the age of 19 that I would one day need His love and guidance as I walked through my share of low valleys that would lead me to the very place I am today. That is the type of God we serve! He is All-Powerful, All-Knowing, Sovereign, and knows the beginning to the end. He is our everything. He is our compass. Without His guidance, we're nothing more than lost sheep without a shepherd.

I am always amazed at how much God loves me when I can be so complicated at times. I would be the first to say that I am not always so sure of what I believed when I couldn't see God working things out on my behalf, which has often caused me to start questioning what I felt I could possibly fix on my own in a realistic timeframe. I didn't want to wait on God's timing. *"He may not come when you want Him, but He'll be there right on time"* was challenging because it pulled on my faith to believe that He was *"able to do exceedingly and abundantly above all that we ask or think, according to the power that worketh in us"* (Ephesians 3:20).

Admittedly, it was His grace and mercy that sustained me through it all. It would be a shame before the throne of God to disrespect Him by discrediting all that He has done for us. If He decided today that He wasn't going to lift another finger to do another thing for us, He would be well in His right to do so because of His unmerited grace and favor that He has bestowed upon our lives. We have so much to be thankful for that we wouldn't be able to muster up enough words to describe just how awesome God is and has been in our lives.

I want you to stop and take a minute to reflect on how you've responded to God this week, last month, or even at a time when you weren't pleased with the plan He had set in place for you. Now, be honest with yourself: Do you need to put this book down and ask God for forgiveness in how you responded to His decision concerning that thing? I'm a fair guy. You can put my book down at any given time and get your life right with God. Again, He is loving and forgiving like that. He will understand. Approach His throne with a pure heart and a mind to do better in learning how to be patient in waiting.

With all due respect, I don't want to deter you from reading this book in its entirety because of the disturbing events that have been mentioned throughout. I do, however, want you to see that through all that has been discussed herein, we serve a mighty God who can do all things and that *"he that cometh to*

The Other Side of Me

God must believe that He is and that He is a rewarder of those who diligently seek Him" (Hebrews 11:6).

I know it gets tough at times when it's unclear as to how the bills will get paid, and the college tuition seems to be a mountain that many of us would love to see decimated. But just like the enemy's obstacles come to serve as roadblocks, we must know these things only serve to make us stronger, build our faith in God, and reassure us in knowing that He's got our back on every hand.

> *"So, do not fear, for I am with you; do not be dismayed, for I am your God. I will strengthen you and help you; I will uphold you with My righteous right hand."*
> **(Isaiah 41:10)**

I believe as a people, that for us to see a great move of God today, it is going to be imperative that we get back to what has carried us through since the very beginning of time—and that's prayer, which has been missing in the body of Christ for a long time now. Without it, how can we survive? The Bible says in John 12:32, *"And I, if I be lifted up from the Earth, I will draw all men unto Me."*

> *"How, then, can they call on the One they have not believed in? And how can they believe in the One whom they have not heard? And how can they hear without someone preaching to them?"*
> **(Romans 10:14)**

In this, God needs to be able to depend on you and me to carry out His tasks. It's not enough to give our lives to Him and never tell others of His goodness and how He has changed our lives. Many people are still lost because many of our so-called "Christians" are still lost due to them not having fully given or submitted themselves to Jesus Christ.

That's why often, the "reprobate mind" comes into play. Many Christians are still living like the world by straddling the fence. The Bible tells us to choose ye THIS day whom we will serve. That scripture requires **ACTION** from us. It demands a lifelong commitment or **CHOICE** be made on our part. If we look at Romans 12:1-2, God lays out the blueprint for our lives by giving us clear-cut instructions to follow a healthy, spiritual lifestyle that is pleasing unto Him.

Romans 12: 1 says, *"I beseech ye, therefore, brethren, by the mercies of God, that ye present your bodies a living sacrifice, holy, acceptable unto God, which is your reasonable* service [your God-given duty]."

Romans 12:2 says, *"And be not conformed to this world: but be ye transformed by the renewing of your mind, that ye may prove what is that good, and acceptable, and perfect will of God* [not easily influenced]."

The truth of the matter is that I had formed a preconceived notion that I would fail in ministry. Others' personal opinions and beliefs of me, whether true or not, made it difficult for me to go out and witness for fear of thinking:

- What if I forget or misrepresent the scriptures by using it out of context?
- What if they turn the cold shoulder on me and reject what I have to say?
- What if they are more intelligent and well-informed and start asking me questions that I have no prior knowledge of?

Remember that 2 Timothy 2:15 instructs us to show ourselves approved unto God by rightly-dividing the Word of Truth unashamedly.

Luke 9:26 tells us that, *"For whosoever shall be ashamed of Me and of My words, of him shall the Son of Man be ashamed, when He shall come in His own glory, and in his Father's, and of the holy angels."*

God gives us an assurance that He will never leave us nor forsake us, no matter what valley we walk in. He makes it clear to us that fear is not an option because He is with us. The "comfort" in this is direct opposition of fear. The "valley of the shadow of death" is a symbolic description of the world, meaning darkness and death are [symbolic] valleys on Earth one must walk through that are a part of the human experience, which leads to conclude that I can do all things through Christ who strengthens me (Philippians 4:13)!

After embracing that revelation, it was and is very clear to me that people are just that: people. Everyone inside and outside of the church isn't always going to agree with what we say or do. It's a fact and simple part of life that makes the world go around. Just think: If we all thought the same and reacted in like manner to the challenges of this world, we would be a "robotic population" of 7.6 billion brainless people with no sense of direction. There would be no need for God, for that matter. What a messed-up world this would be!

I learned that prayer is an opportunity to spend time with God. To truly understand the heart of God, you need to pray. In John 15:15, Jesus says He no longer calls us His servants; He calls us His friends. Talking with God develops a deeper relationship with Him.

Prayer is important because God said, *"If I be lifted up from the Earth, I will draw all men unto me"* (John 12:32). Ephesians 6:18 tells us, *"In the same way, prayer is essential in this ongoing warfare. Pray hard and long. Pray for your brothers and sisters. Keep your eyes open. Keep each other's spirits up so that no one falls behind or drops out."*

Prayer is an act of obedience. God calls us to pray, and we must respond. In doing so, we begin to learn who we are in Jesus Christ. It is vitally imperative that we discover who we are in Him so that we can live life as He intended and fulfill our destiny. The more we identify ourselves with Christ, the more we'll begin to exemplify our God-given identity. Your identity is **NOT** predicated upon what you have or don't have. Your identity is who **GOD** says you are.

If you're unsure of who you are and need answers, try asking God. He knows all because He created all. You don't have to succumb to the slavery of fear. You can get delivered today. In John 10:10, it says that *"The thief cometh not, but for to steal and to kill and to destroy. I am come that they might have life and that they might have it more abundantly."* Once you choose to follow Jesus, you become a new creation. The old you passes away, and you become who you are in Him. You don't have to live out what others say you are. Get into God's Word for yourself, find out what He says about you, and live it out to the best of your ability.

In the event you may need some encouragement, here are a few starter scriptures that will help you along in your journey of getting to know Christ for yourself:

- ❖ "I am loved." (1 John 3:3)
- ❖ "I am accepted." (Ephesians 1:6)
- ❖ "I am a child of God." (John 1:12)
- ❖ "I am Jesus' friend." (John 15:14)
- ❖ "I am a joint heir with Jesus, sharing His inheritance with Him." (Romans 8:17)
- ❖ "I am united with God and am one spirit with Him." (1 Corinthians 6:17)
- ❖ "I am the head and not the tail." (Deuteronomy 28:13)
- ❖ "I am above and not beneath." (Deuteronomy 28:13)
- ❖ "I am the lender, not the borrower." (Deuteronomy 28:12-13)
- ❖ "I am who God says I am." (1 Peter 1:23)

Believe it or not, you're much stronger than you give yourself credit. Once you've truly admitted to God that you need Him and can't continue in the lifestyle in which you've been entrapped, that's when you have opened an avenue for

God to come in and change your life for the better. It is at that very moment when you realize it's just you and God — nothing else matters. It's called the "Secret Place"! That is where the Father desires to dwell within us. In this place, you can cast all your cares upon Him. In this place, you can find rest. It is a "Place of Refuge" where one feels the close presence of the Almighty God. It's where you and I will find love, safety, and security.

Here comes another revelation!

In all of this, I never knew how to get close to God until I was able to talk about it and someone with an actual connection to Him was able to give me sound advice on how to get God's attention and **KEEP** it. Wow! What an amazing and mighty God we serve! I now have hope, peace, and understanding of who God is because I allowed my heart and mind to be opened to what He had for me.

You, my friend, can do the same — if only you allow Him into your heart today.

Never will I paint a picture of a bed of roses as it relates to this Christian walk because it's not. It is a **DAILY** process that leads to our ultimate destiny. We, too, will go through a lot of things — just as Jesus did. That's why He said, *"You will be hated by everyone because of Me, but the one who stands firm to the end will be saved"* (Matthew 10:22). He said he would make our enemies our footstools!

The Other Side of Me

Note: Remember that no man has a Heaven or Hell to put you in. In fact, each will have to answer for his own actions come Judgment Day. We have all sinned and fallen short of the glory of God. It is only by His grace and mercy that we are kept. No sin is greater than the other, just like there are no "little white lies" or "big lies." Each holds equal weight. Each is wrong in God's eyes. So, try not to get so caught up in all of the naysayers' negative hoopla. Only what we do for Christ will last.

We must understand that forgiveness means you've made peace with the pain and are ready to let it go. Forgiveness is not something we do for others; it's something we do for ourselves. Not forgiving someone is the equivalent of staying trapped in a jail cell of bitterness, serving time for someone else's crime.

Whenever my wife and I would argue, I would often shut down out of anger because it was what I did in all of my past relationships. I thought that she was supposed to be different from all the rest. She was supposed to be the one I could talk to about anything. There wasn't supposed to be any signs of regret from marrying her. I started feeling like she had some of the characteristics that my mom and other women in my life had, and that did **NOT** sit well with me. In many cases, I mistreated women and harbored a hatred for them as a way of protecting my feelings and interests. I refused to allow any woman to feel like she had the upper hand in my life.

My wife and I were supposed to be the "ride or die duo" that people modeled their relationships after. However, when I started to see that my wife was a real person with real feelings and a realistic approach to life, she started posing as a threat to me. She wasn't supposed to be **ANYTHING** like my 8-year toxic relationship! She wasn't supposed to be argumentative, self-centered, and selfish! She was supposed to be the young lady I met back in high school, but just like me, she grew up!

That, my friend, was not reality.

I wanted her to be perfect. I didn't want to experience pain from her—or any other woman ever, for that matter. I wanted the pain to be demolished once and for all. In the middle of an argument, I would often give in if I felt like she wanted the conversation to work out in her favor. I would get angry and look for the nearest exit because I didn't want to confront the elephant in the room. I simply wanted out (not out of the marriage, but just to be left alone to deal with my thoughts and anger).

It wasn't until I saw the pain in her eyes as her whole demeanor changed. *"How dare you compare me to your ex or any other woman you've been with!"* she replied. *"I am your wife and would never intentionally hurt you. You know that! I have bent over backwards and gone above and beyond to try to do all that I could for you. Now, I will admit that I don't always come across as sweet and loving as you think I should—and neither do you, but I have never compared you to any of my exes whenever I get upset. You will not continue to disrespect me by comparing me to those **WOMEN!** You've got to stop going from **0-100** in a matter of seconds every time **I SAY SOMETHING YOU DON'T LIKE**. You're my husband and*

The Other Side of Me

I should be able to talk to you about anything. If I can't do that, then you really need to seek help."

For a moment, I stood there shocked that she would blow up the way she did. I watched the tears stream down her face as I tried to conjure up some quick defense. I realized that she was 100% correct in her analogy of me. I could not believe I was doing it again! I was bringing my tainted past to the future of what was supposed to be a new start of something beautiful.

I guess I didn't know how good I had it for her to want to stick around and deal with my mess when she clearly didn't have to. It wasn't like she came looking for me. In fact, she was doing very well for herself and didn't need me coming in and interfering with that. It's not every day that we find someone who's willing to stick around for the long haul to deal with our crap. One thing I do know is that because of her love for me, I will never be the same again. She is my lifelong love and partner and a joy to our entire family as well.

In the end, I found myself asking for her forgiveness as I vowed I would never again make her feel like she was second best. Joann said something to me in the car one day that I will never, ever forget. She said, *"Don't ever preach to me about living right if you haven't learned how to live right yourself."* I was so convicted at that very moment that it left me totally lost for words. What could I say? She was 100% right! I've now become very aware of the things I say to her, especially when I find myself in my feelings.

I now realize that marriage really is work and everything in life isn't always going to be peaches and cream. I learned quickly that Joann wasn't my enemy; she was my wife, my best friend, and the one God saved just for me. Truth be told, I was still hurting and fighting my past.

A lot of my anger and frustration stemmed from my childhood of being told no by my parents when I wanted something or wanted to go somewhere. (Sounds like your typical teenager, huh?) Well, I felt like some of my other siblings were more privileged than me because I was so different from them in so many ways. I was one who had a very low tolerance for foolishness and only dealt with it because I lived in my parents' home. We didn't always see eye-to-eye on a lot of things. You see, my parents owned a lot of real estate, and their sole purpose in life was to buy and renovate the houses for their children to live in and have something they could call their own for the future. I was one who never had an interest in restoring old properties because I had a love for playing instruments and singing. I didn't have a close relationship with my parents because most of their time was spent either at work or putting work into their rental properties.

I'm not trying to paint this huge, horrific picture of my parents as being bad people. They were, indeed, loving people. It's just that their passion and dream weren't my cup of tea. Whether I liked it or not, I was a part of it.

So, through all of this, I felt victimized in the end, only to discover that not all things were going to go my way. That was just the way it was! We don't always get what we want. We must learn that not everything is good for us. People are who they are—good, bad, or indifferent. Some are for you—some aren't. Some love to see you coming—some can't wait for you to leave. It will be that way until the end of the Earth. I've been through enough storms with people to learn how to pick and choose my battles. Some catfights are not worth the time of day, and when you've gone through enough of them, you'll know which ones are even worth the breath you give them.

A lot of people don't have the heart to meet you in the middle. It's all about *"What can you do for me?"* My approach is different. It's *"What are you doing for yourself that would make me want to sow into you?"* I know I have a good heart and mind to help and see everybody prosper, but at some point, we must keep in mind that God helps those who help themselves.

My comeback to those of you who may not necessarily agree with my comment is that I mean no harm, but I don't apologize for why I feel the way that I do. I have gotten so used to sparing people's feelings while being trampled on many occasions. Oh, I can assure you that I am not in my feelings right now. We're just having a heart-to-heart, honest discussion about the things I have ignored throughout my life and now, I am merely hashing them out in a positive manner.

There are so many things I am most grateful for since I first started writing this book. I am thankful for the revelation that God has given me in knowing that I am a child of His and the He loves me unconditionally. Nothing or no one can change that.

Never allow anyone to steal what God has promised you. Always know who you are in Him. Get to know Him for yourself. Walk in the promises He has given you. You must also become selfish in your act of being in covenant with Him. You are to be a witness for Him and always strive to do whatever you can to serve Him in spirit and truth.

I want to ask that you start to take a close self-assessment of where you are in Christ today. Ask yourself the following questions (and answer with all honesty because God already knows **YOUR** truth):

1. Am I in right standings with God?
2. Can I stand to treat my fellow man better than what I already do?
3. Am I living up to my fullest potential or am I merely living from one day to the next, hoping to get whatever comes my way?
4. Was I once motivated at achieving my goals and somehow lost it along the way? If so, what may have caused the downfall?
5. Am I willing to forgive myself and others who have hurt me in the past so that I can get to the place in God where He would have me to be?
6. Am I strong enough to admit to myself and God that I can't live this life without Him?
7. What drives me to be successful or unsuccessful?
8. What am I most fearful of and why?
9. How long will I allow naysayers to control my moving forward?

10. When will I ever forgive myself and realize that the traumatizing incident wasn't my fault? When will I allow healing to take place in my life?
11. When will I stop giving the adversary so much credit for something God may have put in place for my growth and my good so that He may get the glory out of it in the end?
12. When is it time to grow up in God? "When I was a child, I spoke as a child, I understood as a child, I thought as a child; but when I became old, I put away childish things" (1 Corinthians 13:11).

It is imperative that we take on the mindset of Christ. It requires surrendering our hearts and loving Jesus with everything in us. Having the mind of Christ requires faith, developing a mindset on the things of God through a working knowledge of scripture, and an obedient and intimate connection with the Spirit of God.

My wife has told me in conversation that *"faith is something learned; belief comes afterward."* Coming from a Catholic background, she had never experienced a non-denominational Christian life. Obviously, we were cut from different cloths and had varying viewpoints based on what we were both taught while growing up and speaking from our own biblical maturity. Although she had raised some eyebrow-lifting good points, we were both able to conclude that there is only One God, One Faith, and One Baptism.

So, it doesn't matter how you slice the pie! **EVERY** knee shall bow, and **EVERY** tongue shall confess that Jesus Christ is **LORD!**

There Is Life After This

I want to encourage you to take a closer look at your life and see what you can change. What would be most beneficial to add or get rid of? Change is good and often needed in this walk of life. Learn how to love each other, forgive one another, forgive yourself, and be wise in the decisions and choices you make. Realize that we need each other in this world to survive.

I am so blessed to have gone through the challenges in life that proved God had my back all of the time. I've learned how to 'forgive and let go of the past' so that I can live for the future.

If you have dealt with generational curses, decree and declare that the buck stops here and now with this generation. Plead the blood over your family, your children's family, and the generations to come.

Although we can all attest to the fact that life's trials have beaten us down pretty good, at least we can still say that at the end of the day, we are still here, we are still survivors, and whatever didn't kill us made us stronger.

Remember: Life is in the power of the tongue. You can speak life or death over whatever obstacle life may bring you.

We have the power to do all things in Christ because **HE** gave it to us! Why not activate your faith and walk in it?

God has been so good to us. His grace and mercy have sustained us and, in return, He is seeking a people who will serve Him with all of their heart, be key witnesses to sharing His Word, and those who will live a life that exemplifies Him. There is nothing more glorious and sweeter than that.

As I close out this chapter of my life, I want to say that today is the day I free myself from past hurt and pain. I am free in my spirit, and God is doing great things in my life. He has given me a wonderful wife who sticks closer to me than a hand in a glove, an amazing family, and an awesome church home. I am beyond blessed!

****

Thank **YOU** so much for walking this journey with me as I shared with you *"The Other Side of Me"*! I am looking forward to sharing with you Part Two of this book called *Healing After the Aftermath*, which will reveal where we go next after the traumatic drama has taken a toll on our lives.

Be blessed, continue to seek God for direction and revelation, and watch Him do remarkable things in your life! He loves you and wants to change your life—if you let Him ALL the way into your heart today. He died on the cross for our sins so that we can have full access to eternal life with Him.

The Other Side of Me

It is imperative that we understand that God sent His Son into the world to save it, not to condemn it. When Christ died on the cross for our sins, all excuses were nailed to that cross. Therefore, acknowledging that we are sinners opens the door for Him to effect change in our lives. Believing that He died on the cross for our sins and asking Him to come into our hearts to live as our Lord and Savior puts us in a relationship with Him, as we seal it with baptism by water and the evidence of speaking in tongues. Christ is the Way, the Truth, and the Life.

"Let not your hearts be troubled. Believe in God, believe also in Me. In My Father's house are many rooms. If it were not so, would I have told you that I go to prepare a place for you? I will come again and will take you to Myself, that where I am, you may be also."
(John 14:3)

THAT, my friend, is the kind of **GOD** we serve!

Remember: Just like the Prodigal Son had to find his way back home, so did I. What a grand celebration it was after finally making it through the long-tested and awaited journey! I realized all that time, I was missing my first love, Jesus Christ. Just like He waited for me, He's doing the same for you…waiting.

Be blessed, Loves!

See you in the *Healing After the Aftermath* and be on the lookout for my book on relationships called *Will Somebody – ANYBODY – Please Marry Me?*

About the Author

Keith Hughes grew up in Toledo, Ohio. He is a twin and second youngest of thirteen. After graduating from Jesup W. Scott High School, he moved to Cincinnati, Ohio where he attended Cincinnati State and received his Bachelor's Degree in Business Management and Liberal Arts Degree from The Union Institute College.

Keith later went on to seek a career in music and acting, where he worked with some of the greatest R&B and gospel artists to ever grace the stage. He is a singer and musician. He has modeled clothing for many Cincinnati designers and was cast as an extra in the movie "Traffic" with Michael Douglas and

The Other Side of Me

Catherine Zeta-Jones. He played a Roman soldier in the hit stage play "Aida" alongside opera singer Denyce Graves.

Keith has written several wedding songs and plays to include "Moma's Lil' Angel" and "Daddy, Please Don't!" that have appeared in many colleges and churches throughout the Ohio area. He also appeared as a guest Motivational Speaker for the "Step Up Toledo, Inc." broadcast production in Holland, Ohio.

Keith became a middle-school teacher in Cincinnati. Later, he relocated to Jeffersonville, Indiana where he remained until he married and moved back to his native home of Toledo, Ohio. It is there that he and his wife, Joann, are active in ministry and building a new business called "Church Boy Entertainment" ™. They have two grown sons named Adrian and Michael who are their true blessings.

Appendix

Berstein, E. (2011, January 11). Your blackberry or your wife. The Wall Street Journal, D1 & D4. Also available via http://on.wsj.com/gXASsx

`Warren, C. (2009, October 14). Average Internet user now spends 68 hours per month online. Mashable.com via
http://tinyurl.com/linchikwok01122011

www.ingramcontent.com/pod-product-compliance
Lightning Source LLC
Chambersburg PA
CBHW071913110526
44591CB00011B/1663